simply™

chinese
astrology

JONATHAN DEE

A Sterling / Zambezi Book
Sterling Publishing Co., Inc.
New York

Library of Congress Cataloging-in-Publication Data Available

10   9   8   7   6   5   4   3   2

Published in 2006 by Sterling Publishing Co., Inc.
387 Park Avenue South, New York, NY 10016
Copyright © 2006 by Jonathan Dee
Chinese Astrology Illustrations Copyright © 2006 by Tina Fong
Western Astrology Illustrations Copyright © 2006 by Hannah Firmin
Published and distributed in the UK solely by
Zambezi Publishing Limited
P.O. Box 221, Plymouth, Devon PL2 2YJ
Distributed in Canada by Sterling Publishing
C/o Canadian Manda Group, 165 Dufferin Street,
Toronto, Ontario, Canada M6K 3H6
Distributed in Australia by Capricorn Link (Australia) Pty Ltd.
P.O. Box 704, Windsor, NSW 2756, Australia

For information about custom editions, special sales, premium and
corporate purchases, please contact Sterling Special Sales
Department at 800-805-5489 or specialsales@sterlingpub.com.

Manufactured in China
All Rights Reserved

Zambezi ISBN-13: 978-1-903065-50-1
Zambezi ISBN-10: 1 903065 50 X
Sterling ISBN-13: 978-1-4027-2695-8
Sterling ISBN-10: 1-4027-2695-3

contents

INTRODUCTION

Many people ask, "How can Chinese astrology be relevant, because one sign lasts a whole year?" The answer, of course, is that there is more to it than that. Like any other form of astrology, Chinese astrology operates on different levels, and the most basic of these is the study of the animals that rule one's year of birth. A slightly more complex feature involves the yang-yin polarity of the year and the element that rules it. Apart from that, there is the question of which animal governs one's birth moon and the animal that influences one's hour of birth. Professional astrologers in China take into account a great deal more than this, including the day of birth and sometimes the fortnight (two-week period) in the lunar calendar that one was born in, but in this book we'll keep things simple. The good news is that Chinese astrology does not require any complicated calculations. It can provide a shortcut to a greater understanding of yourself, your inner nature, and your destiny.

THE CHINESE YEAR

The first thing you will need to do is to look up your sign according to your year of birth. The Chinese use a lunar calendar, so the start of the Chinese year changes from one year to the next. If you were born in January or February, you must pay special attention to the calendar, because you were born around the time when one sign ends and the next begins. If you were born right on the cusp of two signs, read both and see which fits you best.

Many Chinese are so tuned in to the Chinese calendar that if you say, "I was born under the sign of the Tiger," they would immediately know the year of your birth. They would not remember the actual start date for that year, so they would fall back on a generalized date of February 4, which is sometimes called the "Imperial New Year." Some Chinese astrologers actually prefer using February 4, and that is fine in most instances. However, when someone is born around the time of the New Year, they like to know exactly which sign is really theirs, and with the aid of this book, you can do the job properly for them.

The following list gives the start dates of the Chinese years, each year's polarity (yang or yin, active or passive), its ruling element, and its animal sign.

Year	Start Date	Type	Element	Animal Sign
1930	January 29	Yang	Metal	Horse
1931	February 17	Yin	Metal	Sheep
1932	February 6	Yang	Water	Monkey
1933	January 25	Yin	Water	Rooster
1934	February 14	Yang	Wood	Dog
1935	February 3	Yin	Wood	Pig
1936	January 24	Yang	Fire	Rat
1937	February 11	Yin	Fire	Ox
1938	January 31	Yang	Earth	Tiger
1939	February 19	Yin	Earth	Hare
1940	February 8	Yang	Metal	Dragon
1941	January 27	Yin	Metal	Snake
1942	February 15	Yang	Water	Horse
1943	February 4	Yin	Water	Sheep
1944	January 25	Yang	Wood	Monkey
1945	February 12	Yin	Wood	Rooster
1946	February 2	Yang	Fire	Dog
1947	January 22	Yin	Fire	Pig

Year	Start Date	Type	Element	Animal Sign
1948	February 10	Yang	Earth	Rat
1949	January 29	Yin	Earth	Ox
1950	February 16	Yang	Metal	Tiger
1951	February 6	Yin	Metal	Hare
1952	January 26	Yang	Water	Dragon
1953	February 14	Yin	Water	Snake
1954	February 3	Yang	Wood	Horse
1955	January 24	Yin	Wood	Sheep
1956	February 11	Yang	Fire	Monkey
1957	January 30	Yin	Fire	Rooster
1958	February 18	Yang	Earth	Dog
1959	February 7	Yin	Earth	Pig
1960	January 28	Yang	Metal	Rat
1961	February 15	Yin	Metal	Ox
1962	February 5	Yang	Water	Tiger
1963	January 25	Yin	Water	Hare
1964	February 13	Yang	Wood	Dragon
1965	February 1	Yin	Wood	Snake
1966	January 21	Yang	Fire	Horse
1967	February 9	Yin	Fire	Sheep
1968	January 29	Yang	Earth	Monkey
1969	February 16	Yin	Earth	Rooster
1970	February 6	Yang	Metal	Dog
1971	January 26	Yin	Metal	Pig
1972	February 15	Yang	Water	Rat
1973	February 3	Yin	Water	Ox
1974	January 24	Yang	Wood	Tiger
1975	February 11	Yin	Wood	Hare
1976	January 31	Yang	Fire	Dragon
1977	February 18	Yin	Fire	Snake
1978	February 7	Yang	Earth	Horse
1979	January 28	Yin	Earth	Sheep

Year	Start Date	Type	Element	Animal Sign
1980	February 16	Yang	Metal	Monkey
1981	February 5	Yin	Metal	Rooster
1982	January 25	Yang	Water	Dog
1983	February 13	Yin	Water	Pig
1984	February 2	Yang	Wood	Rat
1985	February 20	Yin	Wood	Ox
1986	February 9	Yang	Fire	Tiger
1987	January 29	Yin	Fire	Hare
1988	February 17	Yang	Earth	Dragon
1989	February 6	Yin	Earth	Snake
1990	January 26	Yang	Metal	Horse
1991	February 14	Yin	Metal	Sheep
1992	February 3	Yang	Water	Monkey
1993	January 22	Yin	Water	Rooster
1994	February 10	Yang	Wood	Dog
1995	January 31	Yin	Wood	Pig
1996	February 19	Yang	Fire	Rat
1997	February 7	Yin	Fire	Ox
1998	January 28	Yang	Earth	Tiger
1999	January 16	Yin	Earth	Hare
2000	February 5	Yang	Metal	Dragon
2001	January 24	Yin	Metal	Snake
2002	February 12	Yang	Water	Horse
2003	February 1	Yin	Water	Sheep
2004	January 22	Yang	Wood	Monkey
2005	February 9	Yin	Wood	Rooster
2006	January 29	Yang	Fire	Dog
2007	February 18	Yin	Fire	Pig
2008	February 7	Yang	Earth	Rat
2009	January 26	Yin	Earth	Ox
2010	February 14	Yang	Metal	Tiger
2011	February 3	Yin	Metal	Hare

Year	Start Date	Type	Element	Animal Sign
2012	January 23	Yang	Water	Dragon
2013	February 10	Yin	Water	Snake
2014	January 30	Yang	Wood	Horse
2015	January 20	Yin	Wood	Sheep
2016	February 8	Yang	Fire	Monkey
2017	January 28	Yin	Fire	Rooster
2018	February 15	Yang	Earth	Dog
2019	February 4	Yin	Earth	Pig
2020	January 24	Yang	Metal	Rat

HOW TO FIGURE OUT YOUR CHINESE HOROSCOPE

Look at your year of birth in the previous table and note down your polarity, element, and animal. For example, for someone born in 1977, the Chinese astrology signs would be yin-fire-snake.

The next thing to do is to figure out your animal moon, which links to your month of birth. This process is even easier because it links with our familiar Western zodiac. For instance, if you happen to be a Virgo, then you were born in the moon of the rooster, and if you are a Sagittarius, then you were born in the moon of the rat.

So someone who was born on June 2, 1982, was born in the year of yang-water-dog, in the moon of the horse. A person born on November 25, 2001, was born in the year of yin-metal-snake in the moon of the rat.

Western Zodiac Sign		Dates	Oriental Moon
♈	Aries the ram	March 21–April 20	Moon of the dragon
♉	Taurus the bull	April 21–May 21	Moon of the snake
♊	Gemini the twins	May 22–June 22	Moon of the horse
♋	Cancer the crab	June 23–July 23	Moon of the sheep
♌	Leo the lion	July 24–August 23	Moon of the monkey
♍	Virgo the virgin	August 24–September 23	Moon of the rooster
♎	Libra the scales	September 24–October 23	Moon of the dog
♏	Scorpio the scorpion	October 24–November 22	Moon of the pig
♐	Sagittarius the archer	November 23–December 21	Moon of the rat
♑	Capricorn the goat	December 22–January 20	Moon of the ox
♒	Aquarius the water bearer	January 21–February 19	Moon of the tiger
♓	Pisces the fishes	February 20–March 20	Moon of the hare

THE ANIMAL HOURS

Just as the animal signs relate to particular years and months, they also correlate with the hours of the day. More precisely, each of the twelve animal signs equates to a two-hour period during the course of twenty-four hours, as seen in chart at right.

There is some discussion as to whether one should use local time at your place of birth or Beijing time, but my research has shown that astrologers in China use local time for everybody. The concept is complicated, because whatever time is added or subtracted to bring the local time into line with Beijing time is then reversed by the amount of longitude between Beijing and the local place of birth. The upshot is that you simply use the time at your place of birth. There is one small proviso, which is that a birth during daylight savings time or British summer time needs to have one hour subtracted. Thus, 1:30 AM becomes 12.30 AM—or the hour of the rat.

Animal Sign	Hours
Rat	11 PM–1 AM
Ox	1 AM–3 AM
Tiger	3 AM–5 AM
Hare	5 AM–7 AM
Dragon	7 AM–9 AM
Snake	9 AM–11 AM
Horse	11 AM–1 PM
Sheep	1 PM–3 PM
Monkey	3 PM–5 PM
Rooster	5 PM–7 PM
Dog	7 PM–9 PM
Pig	9 PM–11 PM

1

YANG AND YIN

So, by now you should know what yearly animal sign you were born under, as well as the element for that year and whether that element is yang or yin. Your Western birth sign should tell you what animal moon you were born under and thus reveal your emotional nature. The hour of your birth (if known) will then show your general temperament and possibly the "face" that you present to the outside world. To understand what all these pieces of information mean, we will have to start with the basics and look at the fundamental concepts of yang and yin.

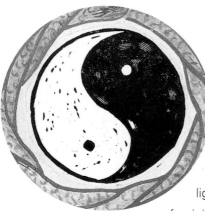

Yang and yin symbol

POSITIVE OR NEGATIVE

Chinese philosophy is based on the idea of balance between the two forces known as yang and yin. Yang is thought of as masculine, positive, light, and energetic. Its opposite, yin, is considered feminine, negative, dark, and passive.

A common error that many people make is to think of yang as "good" and yin as "bad." Nothing could be further from the truth. It is better to think of yang and yin as an interplay of forces, each of which is meaningless without reference to its opposite. These opposites express themselves as day and night, summer and winter, hot and cold, light and dark, and so on, including every pair of conceivable opposites that exist. People too are basically yang or yin by nature. This nature, according to Chinese astrology, is dictated by the polarity of the year in which one was born. If there were no yang-type people in the world, there would be no progress, enthusiasm, sport, exploration, activity, or indeed any change at all. Without yin people there would be no routine and no tasks completed, farms and business would be neglected, children would not be cared for, and tradition and continuity would cease.

Each of the animal signs is considered to be either yang or yin in nature. As one might expect, people born under yang signs are assertive, active, extroverted, and courageous. They may also be inclined to impulsiveness and foolhardiness and be apt to "throw their weight around." People who are born under yin signs are more receptive, patient, subtle, and adaptable. They have the ability to endure, but they may also be prone to negative thoughts and fall prey to depression when times are tough.

Animal	Polarity
Rat	Yang
Ox	Yin
Tiger	Yang
Hare	Yin
Dragon	Yang
Snake	Yin
Horse	Yang
Sheep	Yin
Monkey	Yang
Rooster	Yin
Dog	Yang
Pig	Yin

2

THE ELEMENTS

The elements are at the heart of Chinese astrology and unfortunately are the most confusing aspect of it. There are five elements: wood, fire, earth, metal, and water, and they are always listed in that order.

While each of the twelve animals rules one year, the elements preside over two consecutive years. For example, 1994 was the year of yang-wood-dog, and 1995 was the year of yin-wood-pig. The elements are considered neutral and thus able to change their yang-yin polarity.

The animal signs repeat every twelve years, but they are modified by the change of element within each sequence. To illustrate this point, let us look at the rooster:

1957   Year of the fire rooster

1969   Year of the earth rooster

1981   Year of the metal rooster

1993   Year of the water rooster

2005   Year of the wood rooster

The entire sequence of animal signs and element combinations is only complete when sixty years have passed, so it will not be the year of the fire rooster again until 2017. During each sixty-year cycle, each animal will have been linked with all five of the elements.

In the Western world we tend to place a lot of emphasis on the animals of the Chinese zodiac, but to the Chinese, the five elements are equally important. Traditional Chinese thought holds that the element governing a particular year provides a sort of shorthand to the nature of that year. So a year governed by metal will be thought to be difficult, with more than its fair share of challenges, while a year of the water element will be good for commerce, the economy, and business in general. So ignoring the animal signs for a moment, someone can be described as a wood, fire, earth, metal, or water person.

wood   fire   earth   metal   water

ELEMENTS AND PLANETS

Chinese astrology is no concerned primarily with the heavenly bodies in the same way that Western astrology is, so the following information is only for interest's sake:

- Jupiter is called the wood planet.
- Mars is called the fire planet.
- Saturn is called the earth planet.
- Venus is called the metal planet.
- Mercury is called the water planet.

The sun and the moon are called the "Great Yang" and the "Great Yin," respectively. The outer planets Uranus, Neptune, and Pluto are invisible to the naked eye, so they do not appear in the traditional Chinese system.

Incidentally, the more complex forms of Chinese astrology do involve the study of the planets, the stars, the Milky Way, the moon and its phases and eclipses, and much else that is familiar to Western astrologers and astronomers. However, this more complex information became increasingly confined to a small band of specialists within the emperor's court, and it was kept away from the masses lest they become too knowledgeable. As regimes came and went, some encouraged the use of astrology in court circles and some outlawed it. The result is that true astrology and astronomy became absorbed into the strangely idiosyncratic form that we know today.

THE CREATION CYCLE

The elements are more correctly called "agents of change." They each express a state of being at a particular moment in an ever-changing universe. The ancient Chinese gave them their names because each one reminded them of a particular stage of "change," or, as we would call it, "evolution."

- We begin with wood, which provides fuel for the next element, fire.

- In turn, the remnants of fire, namely ash, go back to the earth.

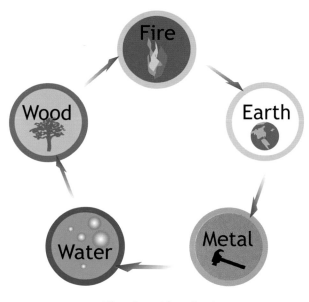

The Creation Cycle

- In the depths of the earth, metal is born.

- Metal when molten flows like water. When metal is in solid form, condensation is likely to form on it, and water is encountered again.

- Water of course is taken up through the roots of plants, some of which form wood.

However, this is not the only way in which the elements can interact. Another sequence has more sinister overtones. Wood can drain earth, earth can befoul water, water can douse fire, fire can melt metal, and metal can chop wood. This is known as the "destruction cycle."

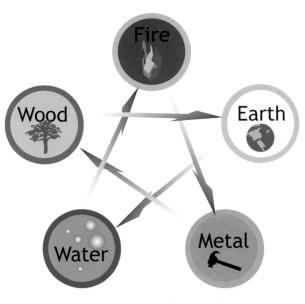

The Destruction Cycle

THE DESTRUCTION CYCLE

These relationships among the elements are relevant to a person's fortunes. For instance, if one were born in a year governed by the wood element, then a metal year would not be very lucky, because metal chops wood. Similarly, a water person would not be too happy in a year governed by earth, because earth muddies water. On the other hand, years that belong to one's own element are said to be lucky.

- Wood exhausts earth

- Earth pollutes water

- Water douses fire

- Fire melts metal

- Metal chops wood

Of course, in the traditions of Chinese astrology, some signs are considered to be compatible, while other signs are counted as enemies. So the prospect of adding an elemental bias also creates another complication. For instance, those born under the sign of the rooster are considered to be compatible with those born under the signs of the ox and the snake. However, if the rooster in question happens to be of the fire element, he will find that an ox or a snake who is of the wood element will tend to encourage him, and this elemental mix will enhance the relationship. This is because wood fuels fire in the creation cycle. On the other hand, our fire rooster is likely to experience a few problems with an ox, who is of the water element, because this ox will tend to dampen the rooster's enthusiasm. The reason for this is because the combination of fire and water form part of the destruction cycle.

The same principle applies to individual years, so an earth-ruled person will not have such good fortune in a wood year (wood exhausts earth). This is an important point to remember, because even if the animal year is compatible with your own sign, its element may not be, and this will moderate the fortunes that you can expect during that year.

On a more positive note, the opposite is also the case. If you find yourself in an animal year that is incompatible with your own sign, then your bad luck may be lessened by that year's favorable element.

• Wood-element people will be happy during wood years because they will be good for them, as indeed will years governed by water or fire. However, earth and metal years are likely to be difficult.

- Fire-element people will find fortune in fire years and also in wood and earth years, while years governed by metal and water will present problems.

- Earth-element people will find that earth, fire, and metal years are more fortunate than water and wood years.

- Metal-element people will find that metal, earth, and water years suit them, while wood and fire years do not.

- Water-element people will be lucky in water, metal, and wood years but not quite so happy in years governed by fire and earth.

THE NATURAL ELEMENTS OF THE ANIMALS

The concept of the natural elements of the animals takes us beyond the scope of a simple book of this kind, but I add it here for your information only.

The ancient Chinese considered each of the animal characters of their zodiac to have a natural inclination toward either yang or yin, and to have a natural preference for a particular element. This despite the fact that each of the signs will, during a sixty-year cycle, experience both polarities and be influenced by each of the five elements. The following list of "preferences" is included here for your information:

- Rat naturally prefers yang and the water element.

- Ox naturally prefers yin and the earth element.

- Tiger naturally prefers yang and the wood element.

- Hare naturally prefers yin and the wood element.

- Dragon naturally prefers yang and the earth element.

- Snake naturally prefers yin and the fire element.

- Horse naturally prefers yang and the fire element.

- Sheep naturally prefers yin and the earth element.

- Monkey naturally prefers yang and the metal element.

- Rooster naturally prefers yin and the metal element.

- Dog naturally prefers yang and the earth element.

- Pig naturally prefers yin and the water element.

3

ELEMENTS AND
WHAT THEY MEAN

At the start of each element, you will find the "correspondences." Some of these will make immediate sense to you, but others will not—until you read books on feng shui, that is. Once you know your element, you can include the colors, shapes, compass directions, and other factors in your home or place of business to make it suit your Chinese element nature and bring you luck. You can even plant the right kind of tree in your garden if you are fanatical enough about such things!

WOOD PEOPLE

Yang year	Oak
Yin year	Willow
Field for yang year	Intellect
Field for yin year	Knowledge
Seeks	Wisdom
Comportment	Achiever
Body shape (yang)	Raw-boned
Body shape (yin)	Slender
Aided by	Water
Hindered by	Metal
Lucky day	Thursday
Lucky season	Spring
Lucky planet	Jupiter (wood planet)
Lucky color	Green
Lucky direction	East
Lucky shape	Rectangle

Those born in periods influenced by the wood element tend to be intellectual. Wood is the element of philosophers, teachers, students, lawyers, and doctors. Education is very important to wood people, and in the modern world, these people are usually inclined toward careers in computing, electronics, science, and communications. Many wood people are deeply interested in philosophical subjects and are inclined to religion and spirituality. Wood tends to impart a clear value system and high standards. This element also implies an influential position and ethical practices. Those born under the wood element will tend to be more compassionate and caring than the characteristics of the year's animal sign might imply.

First Wood-Year Yang
Known as "Oak"

People born in a yang-wood year are very clever and astute. Indeed, there is very little point in attempting to fool them because the motives of others are generally clear to them. Oak-type people are hardworking, responsible, and self-motivated and possess sound judgment. They will thrive anywhere that an organized mind and quick thinking are required. However, they do need to be left to their own devices and to do things their own unique way without interference. In personal terms, it is important to be honest with oak people, because they will not forgive deceit or emotional blackmail.

Second Wood-Year Yin
Known as "Willow"

As the name implies, the willow type of person tends to bend in the wind. These people are extremely impressionable and possess great empathy. It is very likely that willow people will consistently put other people's needs before their own. This trait can cause them to lose out in the long run simply because they didn't pay enough attention to their own interests. Willow people are often shy or modest, rarely asking for recognition. In romance they can be too trusting and often find themselves in a position of vulnerability. In China it is believed that willows are very highly placed in terms of spiritual merit.

FIRE PEOPLE

Yang year	Blaze
Yin year	Flame
Field for yang year	Activity
Field for yin year	Enterprise
Seeks	Fame
Comportment	Showman
Body shape (yang)	Powerful
Body shape (yin)	Wiry
Aided by	Wood
Hindered by	Water
Lucky day	Tuesday
Lucky season	Summer
Lucky planet	Mars (fire planet)
Lucky color	Red
Lucky direction	South
Lucky shape	Triangle

The element of fire was associated with the warriors of ancient China, and their courage makes it easy to see why. Fiery types were also classed as entertainers, acrobats, athletes, and those who staged and took part in public events such as parades. In the modern world, the fire person is also likely to be found in the public eye, in movies, on TV, on the stage, or in the military, fire, or police services. Fire-element people are often crusaders, having made a particular cause their own. Often they will publicly identify themselves with their personal cause, because this element has an association with uniforms, badges, and insignia. Being born in a fire year adds strength, assertion, energy, and passion to the character. However, recklessness and impatience are also likely.

First Fire-Year Yang
Known as "Blaze"

Blaze-type people are warriors who charge at everything. A blaze type is not someone who procrastinates, but someone who gets right to the core of the matter at hand. Blaze types are open and forthright, sometimes uncomfortably so. They are impatient and often possess a "short fuse" and a hot temper. However, they are extremely brave, so if action is needed then a blaze person is the one to call. Blaze-type people are often very clever and quick to pick up new ideas, but their impatience can be their downfall, especially in view of the fact that they don't consider the feelings of those around them and thus can easily make enemies. Traditionally, people born in blaze years make excellent cooks.

Second Fire-Year Yin
Known as "Flame"

People born in yin-fire years provide a steady flame, unlike the fierce conflagration of the blaze type. Flame people are far more likely to be found in the media or on the stage. This type is a performer by nature. Usually less demanding and generally uninterested in adventuring, flame people prefer a glamorous lifestyle, so their uniforms and insignia are unlikely to be military. The flame person is always the center of attention, dazzling his or her audience with personality and witty repartee. However, there is a subgroup of the flame type made up of people who may be smooth-talking con artists who are out to take advantage of the gullible. In general, though, flame people have an instinctive understanding of the public mood and will adapt themselves to appeal to it.

EARTH PEOPLE

Yang year	Grassland
Yin year	Farm
Field for yang year	Industry
Field for yin year	Service
Seeks	Security
Comportment	Still
Body shape (yang)	Stocky
Body shape (yin)	Stocky
Aided by	Fire
Hindered by	Wood
Lucky day	Saturday
Lucky season	The equinoxes
Lucky planet	Saturn (earth planet)
Lucky color	Yellow
Lucky direction	Center, southeast, northeast
Lucky shape	Square

In keeping with the earthy nature of this element, people born in earth years were traditionally held to be excellent builders, farmers, and keepers of water buffaloes. Even in modern times the associations haven't changed much, the areas of expertise being construction, manufacturing, farming, and food production generally. The earth element is a stabilizing influence, adding practicality, business acumen, a generous nature, and often a very long memory. Earth people are patient, prudent, and conventional. The character of an earth-element person is placid and slow to anger but unforgiving of a hurt. However, it does increase the ambition of these efficient souls and grants considerable administrative abilities.

First Earth−Year Yang
Known as "Grassland"

Grassland people, born in the yang-earth year, are generally conventional and in tune with their particular society. They are usually physically strong, possessing a capacity for hard work, and often endowed with a talent for leadership. It is this latter trait that can lead to a position of authority and honor. Grassland types have an honest and down-to-earth manner. They are sensual and "earthy" in sexual affairs. However, they do tend to lack a romantic sense and prefer reliability and stability in relationships over empty but pleasing gestures of affection. Their best opportunities are found in the banking, insurance, finance, and security industries.

Second Earth−Year Yin
Known as "Farm"

All earth-element people are hard workers, and the yin type is no exception. Farm types may project a negative aura of suspicion, but they too will tend to find success in life. Traditionally, this type is supposed to lack imagination, so that they often ignore opportunities if the benefits are not immediately obvious. Farm types are not quite as ambitious as grassland people. In general, farm people prefer to find a comfortable niche in life and then happily stay there for many years. In other words, farm people like being in a rut. On the other hand, many farm people are artistically gifted and express their talents by creating beautiful things.

METAL PEOPLE

Yang year	Steel
Yin year	Ornament
Field for yang year	Management
Field for yin year	The arts
Seeks	Status
Comportment	Graceful
Body shape (yang)	Balanced
Body shape (yin)	Curvaceous
Aided by	Earth
Hindered by	Fire
Lucky day	Friday
Lucky season	Autumn
Lucky planet	Venus (metal planet)
Lucky color	White
Lucky direction	West, northwest
Lucky shape	Oval, circle

Metal people tend to be more independent than other elemental types and unwilling to rely on others. This trait can be seen as an advantage, but it can also make metal types aloof, proud, and too self-contained, so it's important for them to emerge from self-imposed splendid isolation once in a while. Those born in a metal year are determined, unyielding of purpose, and somewhat hard, both on themselves and on others. Metal types are stubborn. Once a course of action is decided on, metal people will stick to it come what may, even when it is obvious that the cause is hopeless. Metal-born people are "a law unto themselves."

First Metal-Year Yang
Known as "Steel"

At first impression the steel person appears to be aloof, a natural aristocrat. Those born in a yang-metal year will easily win respect and admiration but may also tend to put on a few airs and graces because they consider themselves to be a cut above the common throng. As might be imagined, status is very important to this type. Many steel people have something of a head start in life, with families who provided them with all the tools necessary for later success. Even if this is not the case, people of the steel element will progress up the ladder of success very quickly indeed. In affairs of the heart, steel types are as determined as they are in all other arenas, but once their goal is attained they may swiftly cool, become bored, and callously move on.

Second Metal-Year Yin
Known as "Ornament"

The ornament or yin-metal person is as much a natural aristocrat as his or her steel counterpart, but the charm and the "noblesse oblige" that nobility implies is more obvious. This is an idealistic person to whom fair play is very important. Indeed, an ornament person will fight for what is right and often involve him- or herself in social movements and good causes. In affairs of the heart, ornament types can be rather shy, often rather brittle, and tend to avoid commitment. The yin-metal person is thoughtful and will do the right thing, whatever that may be. He or she is capable of making affectionate gestures, but under the shiny metallic exterior really yearns for independence.

WATER PEOPLE

Yang year	River
Yin year	Fishing net
Field for yang year	Liquid assets
Field for yin year	Fixed assets
Seeks	Wealth
Comportment	Flexible
Body shape (yang)	Rounded
Body shape (yin)	Rounded
Aided by	Metal
Hindered by	Earth
Lucky day	Wednesday
Lucky season	Winter
Lucky planet	Mercury (water planet)
Lucky color	Black
Lucky direction	North
Lucky shape	Wavy lines

In Western astrological traditions, the water element is connected to the emotions, but this is not the case in the East. In China the element of water is strongly connected to the idea of communication and to matters of finance and commerce. Traditionally, those born in a water year tended to be tax collectors, merchants, landlords, bankers, accountants, and those who looked after warehouses. Today, that influence is much the same. However, water people are not always successful with money, but if they do lose a large sum, they can usually make it all back again and learn from their previous errors. Apart from their fiscal acumen, water types are intuitive and communicative. Water people can be quite soft and also pretty tolerant. They possess a natural ease of expression and will be envied by other, more socially awkward people. Emotionally, water people are very sensitive and can easily be hurt. They can work so hard that they literally work themselves to death, and they are most likely to do this when they are unhappy in love.

First Water–Year Yang Known as "River"

Those born under the influence of yang-water are clever, talented, hard workers with an eye for opportunity. Indeed, this trait can sometimes be a problem because they never seem to know when to stop working. They possess excellent public relations skills and are natural diplomats, capable of defusing the most difficult situations. River people can spot a gap in the market and then work very hard to fill it. They are also capable of rescuing an ailing business and turning it into a thriving concern. However, romantically, river people can be very fickle. Some can be quite promiscuous. Many of their relationships will feature a notable age gap between partners.

Second Water–Year Yin Known as "Fishing Net"

Fishing-net people are gentle, intuitive, and emotionally vulnerable. However, being of the water element, they still have that ever-present knack for business and finance. The fishing-net type tends to lack an independent streak, so a career in a larger organization would be preferable to charting an individualistic course. This type needs encouragement to thrive. Fishing-net people tend to conceal their true feelings, and this often makes them seem enigmatic. They are extremely romantic people, sincere and loyal in their affections, and very sexy. Many of this type have had a rough time in their relationships and need to develop a more positive self-image.

4

THE RAT

THE RAT

1936, 1948, 1960, 1972, 1984, 1996, 2008, 2020

The Symbolism of the Rat

In contrast to the Western world's opinion of rodents, the rat is considered to be the sign of charm. This is not the vile rat of the sewers but a raider of bulging granaries. The sign symbolized by this opportunistic scavenger is a fortunate one noted for shrewdness, enterprise, and the accumulation of wealth.

The Virtues of the Rat: Charming, protective, dynamic, communicative, compassionate, skillful, upright, attractive, idealistic, prosperous, experimental, talented, adaptable, open-minded, entrepreneurial

The Vices of the Rat: Talkative, obsessive, defensive, addictive, fickle, exploitive, anxious, mean, opinionated, bossy

The Rat Personality

Those born in the year of the formidable rat are shrewd, intelligent, impatient, assertive, and very conscious of their own interests. However, hardworking rat personalities are rarely unpleasant; in fact they are noted for immense charm, social grace, and their excellent sense of humor. Tasteful, refined, and stylish, the popular rat is a person to be noticed. On the more negative side, rats love to gossip; they are very critical both of themselves and of others, and they can be prone to petty attitudes and greed.

It is said that the rat's fortunes will be better if he was born at night or during the summer months. A rat born in the day-time will be less enterprising and more fearful.

The Rat in Love

Rat personalities are extremely devoted to those they love, sometimes obsessively so. This tendency can be taken to extremes, with the rat carrying a flame for someone who does not reciprocate his or her fond feelings. Rats are generous and selfless to those they adore and they do not hesitate to reveal the depths of their feelings. Emotionally, rat types experience many highs and lows in their relation-ships. They are therefore rather fragile and vulnerable. This is because they can be too open about themselves and, while young, may reveal too many personal details to abu-sive types of people. It will take some time, but eventually rat personalities will find the love of their lives, partners who will give them the emotional support and affectionate secu-rity that they crave.

The Rat's Lovers, Friends, and Enemies

The rat is likely to find romance with those born under the signs of the ox, the monkey, and the dragon.

The rat will find companionship with the personalities of tigers, snakes, and pigs, and comfort with other rat personal-ities, even though there will be some friendly rivalry within the relationship. Although the rat and the dog will get along as friends, a marriage between these two would not be wise.

Sheep and horse personalities loathe the rat on sight. Roosters will be irritating to the rat, but with a little give-and-take, the two may tolerate each other eventually.

The Rat Career

Many rats are extremely ambitious and career minded. Energetic, shrewd, and versatile, rats can weave their way through all obstacles and achieve stunning success. Rat personalities are extremely complex, so beneath their veneer of confidence hides a nature that is prone to anxiety—one that cannot accept failure and that fears the mockery of the world at large. This gives a rat person an enormous drive to succeed. Your money should be on the rat, even when he is faced with seemingly appalling odds.

Many rats find fulfillment as writers, and many have a great interest in history.

THE RAT AND THE FIVE ELEMENTS

People born in rat years are also influenced by one of the traditional Chinese elements. This adds a further influence to their already complex personalities.

The Wood Rat (1984)

This wood rat is very shrewd and forward looking. His characteristic insight is such that he or she is aware of upcoming trends and will usually be way ahead of the times. The wood rat is an excellent and eloquent communicator, charming, romantically inclined, and usually artistically gifted. He or she may have known poverty in youth and endured a difficult early life. Security and emotional support are therefore very important to the wood rat.

The Fire Rat (1936, 1996)

The fiery type of rat has a fast, witty, and often caustic tongue. A crusader by nature, the fire rat is never happier than when fighting tooth and nail for a worthy cause. He or she is motivated by very strong ideals and possesses an honorable character. This type longs for excitement and revels in life's dramas. However, when life is dull, the fire rat is usually bored and despondent.

The Earth Rat (1948, 2008)

Money, and lots of it, really matters to the earthy type of rat. This is probably a compensating factor for poverty in early life. These rat types will work very hard to gain security, and they have enough strength of purpose to achieve their ambitions. Their need for security often leads to disastrous early marriages. Later partnerships tend to be better, after earth rats have achieved some prosperity. Only then can they establish a happy family unit.

The Metal Rat (1960, 2020)

This is an idealistic, perfectionist rat. Like his or her fellow rodents, the metallic rat is shrewd in business but may be too conscious of money matters, to the detriment of his or her relationships. The metal rat's emotional life is likely to be turbulent, and he or she may be prone to jealousy. Metal rats often possess an athletic physique, and their innate charm is best distributed over a wide audience.

The Water Rat (1972)

Water rats are intellectual, deep-thinking types who inspire respect. They are diplomats who can cleverly get their own way without offending anyone else. They are a little too critical and their cool exterior can make them appear unfeeling, which is not the case. The water rat is an intrepid traveler but will be happiest when journeying with a good companion who loves and understands his or her complex nature.

THE YEAR OF THE RAT

The year of the rat is the first year of the animal zodiac cycle and it should begin with growing enthusiasm and a sense of optimism. The rat favors the opportunist, so those with the perception to spot a gap in the market should do very well under the influence of this shrewd rodent. In other words, if there is something that you have always yearned to do, but have never found the opportunity to follow your dream, then find time during a rat year! That said, it is not wise to race ahead regardless of consequences. Those who wish to progress will have to prepare for their new enterprise so that it will last beyond the end of the rat year.

The rat is an irreverent creature, so those in authority will find themselves challenged over the course of this year. On the other hand, the creative arts should flourish.

The Fortunes of the Rat Year by Year

The Rat in the Rat Year: When found in its own year, the rat enjoys success and happiness almost beyond measure; no obstacle will be too great for this amorous little rodent. The downside to this good fortune is that all this positive drive and energy may cause the rat to push his or her luck a little too far and receive a short, hard lesson in humility in return!

The Rat in the Ox Year: Hard work is promised for a rat during an ox year, but on the other hand, this enterprising little rodent finds that this is second nature. Even when the struggle becomes a daily grind, rats instinctively know that if they use their heads, projects will have a successful outcome even if the challenges are tough.

The Rat in the Tiger Year: When the rat and the tiger meet head-on, danger and uncertainties result. Situations that were once safe will suddenly become insecure. Being a natural survivor, the rat could still find a path to safety while avoiding the claws of the tiger, but only if the rat learns to use all his or her skills correctly and to the best possible advantage.

The Rat in the Hare Year: In Chinese tradition, the hare is sometimes referred to as the cat, and the rat will have to pit its wits against this feline foe, but these two are evenly matched. It will be a difficult learning curve for the little rodent as it finds itself losing ground to a more cunning and unscrupulous opponent.

The Rat in the Dragon Year: After a couple of difficult encounters, the rat will find a new sense of balance and harmony in the year of the dragon. As long as rats don't try to run before they can walk, they will do well. Fate dictates a year of excitement as new relationships develop, leading to lasting friendships and possibly romance.

The Rat in the Snake Year: The respite offered by the dragon quickly fades when the rat finds itself in the company of the predatory snake. Work and home life will seem increasingly stressful to the rat, who is forced to find a little peace and quiet anywhere he or she can. It is advisable for the rat to remain discreet and truthful in all situations and not to be too trusting. In the snake year, it is vital for rats to keep their wits about them.

The Rat in the Horse Year: If the rat has been prudent, then the year of the horse will be a happy one. If, on the other hand, the rat has squandered previous opportunities to put something away for a rainy day, then the year of the horse will be more difficult. Either way, this is likely to be an expensive time for the rat. Opportunities disappear and commitments mount. The rat will have to rely on natural cunning and swiftness to make the most out of the horse year.

The Rat in the Sheep Year: The creative rat will positively blossom in the year of the sheep! Even the less creative rodents will fare well in this gentle, loving time. Painful memories and past failures will soon be forgotten as the rat moves forward with a new sense of determination and confidence.

The Rat in the Monkey Year: Rats will enjoy a year in the company of the lively monkey. Success is not hard to find and in most cases will just seem to happen spontaneously. Many exciting new situations and opportunities will present themselves in this stimulating year. Rats can finally put the past behind them and enjoy a stress-free time with lots of pleasant surprises.

The Rat in the Rooster Year: When rat meets rooster, the practicalities of life will seem troublesome, and the rat will begin to wonder why he even bothers to keep up the struggle against the world. However, this depressive mood could soon be lifted if the rat keeps both eyes open, as true and lasting love may well be waiting for him.

The Rat in the Dog Year: The everyday struggle and oppressive practical commitments of the previous year are now over, and troubles and difficulties fade away as the rat finally begins to shine. Even so, relationships won't fair so well, and the rat will have to develop a romantic sensibility to devote time and effort to keep the spark of love alive.

The Rat in the Pig Year: This will be a very good year for the rat: bank balances will grow, boosting confidence and leading to a hectic and fun-filled social life. There is every likelihood that this wealth will last, for in the pig year, the rat's destiny is favorable to long-term investments and saving plans that will pay dividends for a long time to come.

5

THE OX

THE OX

1937, 1949, 1961, 1973, 1985, 1997, 2009

The Symbolism of the Ox

The ox is the sign of tenacity and represents enduring prosperity through continuing effort and determination. It is the symbol of the springtime, agriculture, fertility, power, and muscular strength.

The Virtues of the Ox: Patient, contemplative, skillful, dexterous, confident, eloquent, authoritative, industrious, careful planner

The Vices of the Ox: Chauvinistic, proud, petty, critical, eccentric, overly conservative, grumpy

The Characteristics of the Ox Personality

Ox people are traditionally thought to be physically robust and clever with their hands. They are open-minded, practical people who take life in their stride and are seldom disturbed by the unexpected. The ox person likes an orderly existence, free of stress and too much passion. Oxen are home-loving and usually devoted to their families. They are also materialistic, loving comfort, good food, music, art, and comfortable furniture, though this intrinsic materialism and love of comfort is rarely vulgar. Most oxen have excellent taste and will arrange their surroundings superbly. However, some oxen allow the materialistic side of their nature to overwhelm their entire lives, so they can become covetous and miserly.

The Ox in Love

Although ox people are often very clever, they do tend to be a little naive in matters of love. Their cool nature makes it difficult for them to be ardent and demonstrative. However, once they have found a congenial mate who has unearthed and encouraged their innate sensuality, they become completely loyal, faithful lovers who will rarely stray. In oxen relationships, it is continuity rather than passion that counts.

The ox will find happiness with those born in the years of the snake, the rooster, and the rat. Additionally, other oxen will often prove compatible mates.

Dragons, hares, monkeys, and pigs as well as other ox personalities will be good company and supportive friends.

The ox will feel threatened by the ferocity of the tiger. Value-conscious oxen will hate the extravagance of the sheep, be depressed by the pessimistic dog, and be made to feel inadequate in the presence of the extroverted horse personality.

The Ox Career

The ox is a diligent and meticulous worker with an eye for detail and a perfectionist tendency. He or she is happiest in a conventional profession, one with a recognized, traditional structure and a clear-cut system of promotion. Preferably this is a career that has titles such as "department head", "manager," and "executive director." Oxen are particularly suited to estate management, gardening, farming, medicine, and religion. Oxen could also be cut out for a career in teaching, catering, or the police force.

THE OX AND THE FIVE ELEMENTS

People born in ox years are also influenced by one of the traditional Chinese elements. This adds a further influence to their already complex personalities.

The Wood Ox (1985)

The wood ox is an ox who is ethical above all else. He or she will be renowned for honest dealings and integrity. The wood element predisposes this ox to possess social graces and to be thoughtful, considerate, and kind. The wood ox is a deep thinker but is not afraid of new ideas. In fact, many of this type's ideals are progressive. In material terms the wood ox is capable of attaining great wealth.

The Fire Ox (1937, 1997)

The fire element adds charisma to the ox personality. This is an ox who is drawn to the heights. Ambitious and possibly ruthless in attaining his aims, the fire ox is proud and will be determined to get his or her own way. The fire ox will find it easy to dismiss opposition as the envy of inferiors. To be fair to the fire oxen, though, they are hard workers and are scrupulously honest and direct.

The Earth Ox (1949, 2009)

The earth ox is a very practical type. Sincere, hardworking, practical, and very loyal, the earth-ox person has a strong sense of purpose and will persevere through all sorts of difficulties with a dogged determination, and without complaint, to finally arrive at the desired goal. The earth ox may lack imagination and might be considered unemotional, but he or she possesses a good heart nonetheless. The earth ox's main fault is obstinacy.

The Metal Ox (1961)

The metal ox is an extremely proud, often arrogant, type of ox. Extremely strong willed, with a tough, determined character, the metal ox is not afraid of challenges and will give as good as he or she gets in confrontations. Early life is likely to have been difficult for this type, and early challenges will have given the metal ox a tough hide.

The Water Ox (1973)

The best description of a water-ox person is one who enjoys material comfort but suffers from emotional impoverishment. This is a realistic ox who makes the best out of even the worst circumstances. The water ox is patient, calm, and reasonable. He or she is industrious and works well with others. Unfortunately, the water ox may be jealous and suspicious in love.

THE YEAR OF THE OX

The sequence of the animal signs enters a stable phase in the year of the ox. However, this is not an easy ride, for the ox teaches us the value of hard work as well as the important lesson that we get the rewards of life in direct proportion to the efforts we put into it. So, the lazy, feckless people who have wasted previous opportunities will not be too happy as the world suddenly becomes a more demanding place. This is a good year to make advantageous contractual agreements. This also implies that it is an excellent year in which to get married. The general rule governing the ox year is this: if your plans have been well thought out and arrangements made previously (in the year of the rat), then all will be well. Spur-of-the-moment decisions are not so favorable. Slow and steady progress is the hallmark of the ox year, so patience is required. The results will be worth waiting for.

The Fortunes of the Ox Year by Year

The Ox in the Rat Year: A sense of companionship prevails in the rat year as the ox finds him- or herself in the presence of people with whom he or she has much in common. However, these new bonds are unlikely to develop into romances. Intellectual relationships are favored, and the oxen will find much to occupy their minds. Reunions with old friends are likely. There is plenty of work to be done in this period, but this work will be undertaken with a cheerful heart.

The Ox in the Ox Year: The ox is well placed in its own year and will enjoy a carefree time of happiness and joy. The usual pressures of mundane life will seem insignificant in this onslaught of positive energy. The usually steady and dependable ox may now be tempted to take a few risks, but this uncharacteristic behavior will soon pass, allowing the ox to make some far-reaching decisions that will continue to pay dividends well into the future.

The Ox in the Tiger Year: This is not the best of years for oxen. Complications will arise in all areas of life, and major changes may occur as a result. Confusion and indecision may be rife, and all the ox can do in the face of adversity is to knuckle down and work on the things that are really important in life.

The Ox in the Hare Year: The ox and the hare quickly grow bored in each other's company. The ox should try to avoid any close relationships during this year, especially those with colleagues, as this may lead to irritation and feelings of inadequacy because others may seem to be stealing the glory. A change of image might help; a change of attitude certainly will!

The Ox in the Dragon Year: Another uncomfortable time is forecast when the ox spends a year in the company of the dragon. Tension and stress take their toll as the persistent ox finds him- or herself in a struggle against the ostentatious dragon, and it's unlikely that the ox will win, at least in the early stage of the conflict. However, dogged determination will pay off in the end, because even the dragon will tire eventually. It would be best for the ox to consider long-term goals rather than immediate ones, because the more distant goals are more likely to be achievable.

The Ox in the Snake Year: The ox finds comfort in the company of the snake. Happiness and contentment will return as life takes on a steadier, more manageable pace. Finances will improve, and a clever ox will find time to put something away, and even make a considerable profit. The only fly in the ointment is that the evidence of the good life might be found in an expansion of the waistline!

The Ox in the Horse Year: Hard work and persistence will really pay off in a big way for the ox in the year of the horse. Rewards for past efforts will be gratefully received as fate smiles sweetly on the ox. He or she must ensure that complacency doesn't set in and must be prepared to make a sudden decision if he or she is to take advantage of the maximum opportunities available. Remember that if the ox is too slow off the mark, he or she could be left behind.

The Ox in the Sheep Year: Because the ox and the sheep are both grazing animals, you might be fooled into thinking that this will be a happy time for the ox, but not so! Life will take on a dreamy feel. Things will seem indistinct and somehow unreal, leaving the ox with an uncharacteristic sense of vagueness. The ox must resist all urges to delay or to fantasize this year, or he or she will experience one problem after another.

The Ox in the Monkey Year: Fortune should be generally quite good for the ox during the year of the monkey, but the straightforward-thinking bovine will occasionally struggle to adapt quickly enough to rapid changes. A positive mental attitude will be very important in times of stress. Luckier oxen may be blessed with an exciting new love affair.

The Ox in the Rooster Year: The ox will feel immediately at home in the company of the rooster, as stability, order, and progress are the watchwords during the year of this strutting fowl. The ox's staid image may finally be dumped as the outgoing nature of the rooster rubs off on the rather old-fashioned and conservative ox, but be warned not to take this trend too far, as personal and intimate relationships may suffer!

The Ox in the Dog Year: The personality of the ox might feel the urge to migrate to pastures new. The desire to expand horizons will now be irresistible, and it is a wise ox who will follow his or her instincts. This outgoing, adventurous urge provides a necessary next step on life's pathway, for wherever it leads will be better than the circumstances that have been left behind.

The Ox in the Pig Year: Things speed up for the ox as it chases the pig. But the ox finds an ally in the sentimental pig, and relationships, whether personal or professional, will prosper as the pace of life picks up. Expect a few raised eyebrows, as friends might be shocked to see how the image of the ox is transformed in the pig year. The ox should now indulge his or own desires without worrying too much about other people's opinions.

6

THE TIGER

THE TIGER

1938, 1950, 1962, 1974, 1986, 1998, 2010

The Symbolism of the Tiger

The tiger is the sign of courage. Chinese tradition states that this ferocious beast received one stripe on his back for every animal that he defeated. The tiger is symbolic of the West, the evening, and the harvest. The mighty tiger represents optimism, humanitarianism, and valor.

Virtues of the Tiger: Lovable, alluring, warm-hearted, honorable, independent, idealistic, humanitarian

Vices of the Tiger: Rash, hotheaded, reckless, quarrelsome, caustic, moody, rebellious, disobedient, irreverent

The Tiger Personality

Those born in the year of the tiger are fascinating personalities. The tiger person is vain, sociable, kind, humorous, and cheerful, but never make the mistake of thinking that the tiger is gullible or a fool. The tiger's flippant facade conceals a wild and ferocious nature. Tigers have inner strength and enormous ambition. They will never be content to put up with second best. Tigers always have their eyes on the top! They love wealth and status, but they are also rebellious and won't be able to abide the authority of anyone else for very long. Tigers work hard and live hard. Their energies are awesome. They have expensive tastes, so it's a good thing that they also have the capacity to make a lot of money. Unfortunately the typical headlong rush of the tiger has its price. Tigers are prone to stress-related ailments if they don't take the demands of their bodies seriously enough.

The Tiger in Love

The tiger personality is pleasure seeking, with enthusiasm for life and a love of variety. Therefore, with so much to offer, it is not surprising that the tiger can be a fickle lover. He or she falls in love a thousand times and on each occasion says, "This is the one!" And it is, until boredom and predictability set in and the relationship becomes routine. Then it is time for the tiger to roam again. However, people of independent character will attract the tiger, especially those who play hard-to-get. In essence, the tiger needs a quietly admiring partner, one who is steady, consistent, practical, and very understanding.

The tiger may form fulfilling relationships with those born in the years of the dragon, horse, and dog.

The adventurous tiger will win popularity with rats, hares, roosters, pigs, and occasionally other tigers.

However, the cautious ox, the guileful snake, and the chattering monkey are threatened by the tiger's bluster and will tend to avoid him or her.

The Tiger Career

Tigers are optimistic, determined, and filled with initiative, so they constantly seek novelty and challenge in their work. A tiger person is most often self-employed or runs his or her own business. However, any career that involves a variety of activities will win favor from the tiger, especially if he or she is to be found in a leadership capacity. The tiger has a talent for inspiring loyalty and the best effort from subordinates, so the typical place to find the tiger personality is in a position of authority.

Tigers are particularly suited to careers in the travel industry, design, advertising, or politics. Tigers are often drawn to a military life. They may become explorers, travel writers, journalists, or captains of industry.

THE TIGER AND THE FIVE ELEMENTS

The five traditional Chinese elements also have an influence on the character of the ferocious tiger.

The Wood Tiger (1974)

Wood-tiger personalities love prominence and celebrity, often finding themselves in a position of great responsibility, whether they wanted to be or not! This type of tiger is often so independent-minded that he or she prefers to live alone. Usually creatively gifted, artistic, original, and inventive, wood tigers will earn a respectable income and a considerable reputation. Family life may be a problem, and an emotional distance with parents may emerge.

The Fire Tiger (1986)

The fire tiger is an extremely devious person. He or she is very, very clever—perhaps a little too clever, because his or her intricate plots and manipulation of others can backfire quite spectacularly. The fire tiger possesses a vast range of general knowledge and, like most tigers; the fiery type enjoys the limelight and the company of celebrities. Fiery tigresses are sexually passionate and fiercely loyal. They are, however, possessive and prone to jealousy.

The Earth Tiger (1938, 1998)

Earth tigers are resourceful and hardworking tigers. They have had to be! In most cases, earth tigers have had a difficult early life. This type usually leaves home young and claws his or her way up the ladder of success. This is a person with excellent leadership qualities. He or she possesses sound judgment and is capable of inspiring loyalty. In relationship terms, the earth tiger is faithful and possessive.

The Metal Tiger (1950, 2010)

The metal tiger dominates those around him, but he or she may lack empathy and has a reputation for being constantly dissatisfied. There is no doubt that the metal tiger is very lucky, especially with money, but he or she is rarely content with his or her good fortune. This is an egoistic tiger, witty, eloquent, and passionate. This type is likely to be a risk taker and a gambler. Some metal tigers make millions, but they must take great care not to squander their fortunes.

The Water Tiger (1962)

The water tiger will gain a reputation for honest dealings in business and fickleness in love. This is a born businessperson, resourceful, ambitious, and persuasive. However, the water tiger has difficulty ending situations and moving on, so old problems often return at inconvenient moments. This tiger is in particular danger when beginning a relationship without ending a previous liaison.

THE YEAR OF THE TIGER

The twelve months governed by the ferocious tiger could easily be described as the "year of living dangerously." The arrival of this fearsome jungle cat heralds a turbulent time, so it's not easy for timid souls to live through it without experiencing a lot of anxiety. For those who desire a quiet life, it's best to sit tight and hope for the best as the storm rages. Those who will do best in this frantic year are people who abandon logic and cool, calm planning and rely on intuition. Those who act in an impulsive manner and are willing to take a risk will also tend to do well, simply because they are in sympathy with the adventurous tiger nature. For this year it's best to keep an open mind, take each day as it comes, and, catlike, be ready to pounce in any direction at a moment's notice.

The Fortunes of the Tiger Year by Year

The Tiger in the Rat Year: Money and resources will be something of a problem for tigers in the rat year. It's time for the tiger to tighten his or her proverbial belt. The rat is far too practical to be swayed by a tigerish revolutionary zeal, so it is important to retain a sense of proportion, be sensible, and if possible, try to put something away for a rainy day!

The Tiger in the Ox Year: Another difficult year is forecast when the tiger and the ox meet. Arguments and conflicts will be rife, simply because the tiger is prone to overconfidence and is likely to charge into a fight without considering the possibility of losing. And losing is a very likely outcome! The tiger must think twice, because sometimes it is better to bite one's tongue and bide one's time.

The Tiger in the Tiger Year: It is said that what the tiger does in his or her own year will stay with the tiger for the next decade. Whatever the tiger chooses to do now, fate will be kind and flexible, allowing the tiger to make long-term plans. This is a particularly good time for following romantic inclinations. Marriages and relationships are especially well starred when the bold tiger hunts in his or her own year.

The Tiger in the Hare Year: The seeds that the tiger planted in his or her own year will start to sprout and flourish in the year of the hare. In the race of life, the tiger will swiftly move ahead of all others. But a note of caution should be sounded, because a boastful, show-off attitude won't help tigers to win friends and influence people, so it is best if they are a little more modest about their achievements.

The Tiger in the Dragon Year: The tiger and the dragon have much in common, but even so, it's important for the tiger to know his or her place. After all, this is the dragon's year, and the wiser tiger will acccpt this and be content to play second fiddle. In other words, don't rock the boat. As long as he or she is professional and businesslike, the tiger will find a way to prosper in this year!

The Tiger in the Snake Year: This will tend to be a frustrating year for the tiger. Everything seems to slow down, as life, like a sluggish river, meanders across a plain. All the tiger can do is to sit back and go with the flow. Taking a little time out will help the tiger to unravel his or her fraught nerves and to learn to relax a little and appreciate life more fully.

The Tiger in the Horse Year: This will be a very good year for the tiger. All areas of life will improve beyond the tiger's reasonable expectations. Even though things are going well, it is a wise tiger who ignores the urge to take big risks or show off. This year, the tiger should work hard and enjoy his or her good fortune without letting success go to his or her head!

The Tiger in the Sheep Year: The tiger's revolutionary zeal will fall out of favor in the year of the sheep. The tiger will tend to stand out for all the wrong reasons, leading to misunderstandings and feelings of alienation. In this year it's best if the tiger sits back and takes note of developments going on in his or her environment. Tigers must learn patience and wait until their individualistic style is more in vogue!

The Tiger in the Monkey Year: Fortunes will improve for the tiger in a year filled with dramatic twists and turns.

Revolutionary ideas will become more fashionable, putting the tiger back in control. Whatever the creative tiger can imagine will be achievable during the monkey year, and it may be that only the tiger's vision could possibly imagine where it will all lead!

The Tiger in the Rooster Year: The tiger's social life will receive a boost during this year. Any problems occurring now will tend to be minor and short-lived. Even though the practicalities of life are not to the fore in the rooster year, tigers will sort out a lot of petty irritations. It is in the area of romance that tigers will "burn bright"; relationships, both long- and short-term, will be very fortunate for the tiger in this year!

The Tiger in the Dog Year: The year of the faithful dog is auspicious for the tiger. Revolutionary ideals will once again find favor. In career terms, the going might be challenging, yet the tiger will cope with this and even prosper as his or her innovative thinking will solve problems and increase productivity. In addition, tigers will still find time to focus on long-term friendships and relationships.

The Tiger in the Pig Year: Tigers will develop a more easy-going nature during the happy-go-lucky year of the pig. It's inevitable that some standards will drop as the tiger's finances shrink while other people seem to prosper, but this is nothing to worry about. The wiser tigers will realize that this trivial setback is a minor phase of life and will eventually end. Tigers should use this time to experience a little more of life!

7

THE HARE

THE HARE

1939, 1951, 1963, 1975, 1987, 1999, 2011

The Symbolism of the Hare

The hare is considered to be the sign of virtue. It represents longevity, high standards, and prudence. The legendary Chinese character of the hare on the moon is said to be always busy grinding the ingredients of the elixir of immortality with a mortar and pestle. The Buddha is believed to have taken the form of a hare in one of his previous incarnations.

The Virtues of the Hare: Sensitive, refined, tactful, prudent, cultured, creative, considerate, gracious, discreet, and long living

The Vices of the Hare: Pedantic, haughty, self-indulgent, hypochondriacal, judgmental, condescending, self-righteous

THE HARE PERSONALITY

Hares are refined and fastidious creatures, and their good taste is shared with those born under this sign. Some hare personalities are quite aloof and snobbish, but that is not a universal characteristic. Hares are often reserved, preferring to stand back from the common throng, but that does not always mean that they consider themselves to be superior. They are good at creating an impression that they are imaginative, self-assured people with cool, emotional detachment. In fact, this is an expression of their highly strung, sensitive natures. In short, hare people tend to get very upset by confrontations and dramas unless they cause them, in which case they can quite enjoy the chaos they create.

Hare people often possess great intelligence, interesting looks, and a reserve and refinement suggesting an aura of mystery. In addition, the observant hare is often extremely intuitive—often psychic.

The Hare in Love

There are only two ways that others can react to the hare person: with respect and admiration, or with respect and loathing, but always with respect! In relationships, it is vital to remember that although the facade of the hare is impressive, it conceals a deep sense of inadequacy. A threatened hare will react to hostility by either raging wildly or, even worse, cutting an opponent to the quick with cold sarcasm and then quickly retreating.

Hares desperately need tenderness, understanding, trust, and security within a close relationship. The easily frightened hare will shy away from brash types but may be wooed by quiet sincerity and persistence.

The hare is likely to find love with the artistically gifted sheep, the sensitive pig, and the loyal dog.

The horse, snake, ox, and tiger will develop into friends, but for real mutual appreciation, try another hare!

The hare will sense a threat from the ostentatious dragon, and his or her sense of refinement will be appalled by the forthright candor of the rooster and the overt charm of the rat.

The Hare Career

With such refined sensibilities as a part of their personalities, it is not surprising that many hare people are artistically gifted, so any career that involves an expression of personal flair and good taste will find favor with the hare. Hares would not enjoy the rough and tumble of business life or a career with too much pressure. They prefer to work at their own pace in a methodical manner.

One may find the hare in such diverse careers as writer, librarian, artist, designer, or diplomat. Hares excel at public relations and may also consider the law, becoming an attorney, judge, or a court recorder.

THE HARE AND THE FIVE ELEMENTS

The five ancient traditional Chinese elements give extra variations to the hare character.

The Wood Hare (1975)

The wood-hare personality is conventional, intelligent, quiet, and modest. Wood hares possess a compassionate nature, which often leads them to help others who are less fortunate. If they can accomplish this charity work in an anonymous, or at least an unobtrusive fashion, so much the better. They may excel in the fields of athletics or writing.

The Fire Hare (1987)

Artistic temperament is found in the fire-hare personality. This hare is likely to be highly strung, eccentric in habits, emotional, and intuitive bordering on the psychic. The medical professions appeal to some, but others are drawn to healing with alternative therapies. Fire hares are cheerful, popular, and fun loving, devoted to their families. Security is vital in their relationships, and the same applies to the way they handle finances.

The Earth Hare (1939, 1999)

This is an extremely logical hare, one who holds to sound common sense in all dealings. The earth hare is not very ambitious and is generally reliant on someone close who is altogether tougher and more pragmatic. This is an easygoing hare who wants to lead a quiet, ordinary life. The earth hare is careful with money and devoted to conventional family values, believing that a sound education is the foundation of the future.

The Metal Hare (1951, 2011)

This hare is likely to be a connoisseur, a collector, or if one is to be harsh, a hoarder! The metal type can be considered to be moody, but he or she actually needs periods of solitude. However, this does not make the metal hare a hermit—far from it, as the sincerity of the metal hare wins influential friends and allies. Emotionally, this hare is possessive and in general very protective of friends and family.

The Water Hare (1963)

The water hare is an artistic dreamer. This type is sensitive, romantic, very caring, and so emotional that he or she is easily upset. Unusually for the hare personality, this type doesn't seem to mind financial insecurity as long as he or she is allowed creative expression. The water hare loves to travel and often entertains with imaginative tales of his or her adventures. Not an ambitious type, the water hare is usually content with the possessions in hand.

THE YEAR OF THE HARE

The year of the gentle hare will come as a relief after the turbulence of the tiger year. Traditionally, the hare year is thought of as a time of peace and harmony when hostilities should cease and rebuilding should begin. Of course this relatively quiet period will not suit everyone. Those who wish to race ahead with their plans,will find this period frustrating. To those who have been stressed, this is a welcome time, notable for an easing of pressure and a return to tranquillity. The charitably minded will do best this year. Those who put the interests of others before their own are likely to do very well, even though that is not their intention. This year is also good for family life. It is considered to be excellent for marriage and for increasing the size of the family.

An upturn in the world's financial markets is to be expected in the year of the prudent hare, so excellent investments and profits are possible. In the creative sphere, innovation in fashion and some masterworks in the arts and media are to be expected.

The Fortunes of the Hare Year by Year

The Hare in the Rat Year: This will be a year filled with peril and pitfalls for any hares who do not keep their wits about them. There are far too many possibilities for deception and hidden dangers for the hare. Senses should be sharpened if the hare is to find his or her way through the traps and lies of false friends who have but one motive, to part the hare from his or her hard-earned cash!

The Hare in the Ox Year: The year of the diligent ox provides plenty of challenges for the hare as well as teaching some hard lessons. Attention must be paid to the less glamorous aspects of life. Hard work and the mundane practicalities of life will take over now. Even so, hares should not dread this year because they will learn much about themselves as well as adding to their life experience.

The Hare in the Tiger Year: A year of revolutionary changes is forecast when the hare meets the tiger. It is fortunate that the fierce tiger is a friend of the hare and will help him or her to adapt in this time of upheavals. It is more than likely that the hare will weather the storms that overwhelm others and eventually profit from this turbulent time.

The Hare in the Hare Year: It is an extremely fortunate time for the hare during its own year. Past troubles will be forgotten as the hare looks to the future with a new sense of hope and adventure. Luck will be with the hare, and although a little risk-taking might pay off initially, it's important to take care of money because there is a possibility that less scrupulous folk may try to take advantage of the hare's good nature.

The Hare in the Dragon Year: The outgoing exuberance of the dragon will disturb the quiet refinement of the hare. The naturally philosophical hare will just have to learn to lay low and avoid the turmoil that is a constant feature in the lives of those nearby. At least the hare knows instinctively when it is time to "go to ground," and some discretion as well as some fancy footwork might be in order this year!

The Hare in the Snake Year: This is a great year for hares, as they can follow their intellectual nature and take some classes or enter higher education. This might lead to criticism and certain problems within friendships, however, simply because it would be too easy for the hare to develop a superior attitude, becoming aloof and selfish. Remember that the whole point of the exercise is to pursue a better understanding of the world.

The Hare in the Horse Year: The pace will pick up for the hare during this year, but the hare will cope well with this increase in speed and will deal with all that the world can put in his or her place. The only source of worry might be the hare's tendency to become involved in other people's problems. This would not be a good move, so it is best if the hare attends to his or her own concerns and develops a certain reserve and emotional distance.

The Hare in the Sheep Year: The sheep is a compatible sign with that of the hare, so this year is likely to be a good one. Even though, in the early months of the year, the money situation could be better, the hare will still manage to enjoy the finer things in life and develop new and stimulating friendships. The hare will naturally seek out the company of like-minded people who will appreciate his or her refined qualities.

The Hare in the Monkey Year: Life seems to descend into chaos in the year of the chattering monkey. Other people will constantly change their minds and act in a strange, disconcerting manner. This will prove to be an anxious time for the gentle hare personality, and the best thing that he or she can do is stand aloof and, if possible, well away from more excitable people. Smarter hares will hide and use this time to follow more intellectual pursuits.

The Hare in the Rooster Year: The year of the rooster is not favorable for the hare's financial fortunes. It is likely that the cash flow will dry up to a slow trickle, and it is too easy for the hare to fall prey to anxiety. Sudden and unexpected problems will plague the hare, and the best thing to do is lie low and let the world move on without one. The hare must avoid moneymaking schemes, as they could prove to be very costly.

The Hare in the Dog Year: After the worrying experiences of the rooster year, the naturally sensitive hare can be excused if he or she is still looking for problems around every corner as the year of the dog dawns. However, problems this year are unlikely to be external, and the hare's own anxiety and paranoia are the only real difficulties to be encountered. As time passes, the hare will relax as life finally settles down to a more comfortable pace.

The Hare in the Pig Year: The hare will breathe a sigh of relief as the year of the pig comes around. Fate will smile on the hare now, as both romantic and financial good fortune have arrived. The welcome injection of extra money will boost the hare's social life. The hare might even have a total image change. Hares should get out and about to see a little more of the world. Many will meet a new love interest somewhere along the way.

THE DRAGON

THE DRAGON

1940, 1952, 1964, 1976, 1988, 2000, 2012

The Symbolism of the Dragon

The dragon is considered to be the sign of good fortune. It has been used as the heraldic emblem of the Chinese emperor and, in a more general sense, of China itself. This powerful mythic creature symbolizes the inexorable course of destiny and the forces of nature.

The Virtues of the Dragon: Magnanimous, charismatic, principled, accomplished, good-hearted, wise

The Vices of the Dragon: Bombastic, dissatisfied, ruthless, demanding, opinionated, egocentric, willful

The Dragon Personality

A person born in the year of the exhibitionist, enthusiastic, and demanding dragon will be outspoken, versatile, resilient, energetic, stylish, and proud. The dragon type is lively and will have a natural charisma and never, ever fade into the background or be ignored. Dragon people are confident. They believe in themselves and possess very high standards, demanding perfection both from themselves and from others. This trait is often mistaken for arrogance. However, dragon people will always act with good intentions even if their tact is somewhat lacking.

The Dragon in Love

Even though dragons possess high principles, they have a very individual way of expressing their honorable intentions, especially in affairs of the heart. Their precious moral code may be moral only in their own opinion, and not that of the society that they inhabit. Dragon people often display a promiscuous streak in their nature and are capable of maintaining multiple relationships. Woe betide any lover who is too emotionally dependent or jealous, because they will find themselves swiftly, and sometimes ruthlessly, dumped! That said, the dragon will retain the affections of ex-lovers long after the flame of passion has gone out.

Those most romantically compatible with the charismatic dragon are born under the signs of the monkey and the rat. However, both the rooster and the snake will find dragon charm irresistible.

On a more platonic level, the dragon person will be happy and intellectually stimulated in the company of the tiger, pig, and sheep.

However, neither the dog nor the ox will be in sympathy with the exuberant dragon personality. Ancient tradition has it that "the dragon flies to the clouds at the sight of the hare." Two dragons together will tend to be extremely competitive and quarrel frequently, so there is little chance of happiness with those of their own sign either.

The Dragon Career

Dragon people are lucky, courageous, intelligent, and capable. It follows that dragons are risk takers who have no patience with the cautious, slow, long-term approach to business matters. Ambition is the great driving force for dragons, and they will not allow anyone to thwart their plans. They exude authority, which most people will take at face value. They excel in fields in which a display of panache and flair are required, but if they can develop an attention to detail, then their ultimate success is ensured.

THE DRAGON AND THE FIVE ELEMENTS

Each of the five elements of Chinese tradition adds a further level of interpretation to the dragon character.

The Wood Dragon (1964)

The wood dragon is logical, inventive, and creative but often eccentric. Although they are ardent lovers and desire admiration, wood-dragon people are often too independent to settle down and prefer to live alone. A person born in the wood-dragon year will have a comfortable lifestyle, will enjoy life, and can look forward to a happy old age.

The Fire Dragon (1976)

The fire dragon is competitive, outspoken, and argumentative, determined to get his or her own way! This forthrightness may sound unappealing, but it is actually attractive, and like all dragons, the fire type possesses considerable charm. One is never bored in the company of this adventurer. However, fire dragons tend to be self-absorbed and prone to accidents.

The Earth Dragon (1988)

Earth dragons just know that they are right . . . about

everything! Infuriatingly, they usually are. To be fair to them, they are truly gifted and outstanding, probably destined to move among influential people. When seeking a mate, they should marry for love, for then they will achieve great fortune. However, should they make the mistake of marrying for status or money, then disaster will strike them and their loved ones.

The Metal Dragon (1940, 2000)

Metal dragons love material wealth and the high life. They may be a little too obsessed by status and they can fall prey to envy. They are blunt and forceful in their opinions, but they remain charming. The one truly negative trait ascribed to metal-dragon personalities is that they are thought to be tight-fisted. In short, they are considered mean!

The Water Dragon (1952, 2012)

The water-dragon personality is extremely faithful, intelligent, and honorable. The arrogance of the dragon is still evident, and water dragons will refuse to be advised in any matter. These dragons are great readers and are often very learned. Female water dragons are often drawn to psychic or spiritual matters. Water dragons of both genders are not complete unless they have a soul mate who truly appreciates them.

THE YEAR OF THE DRAGON

The year of the dragon is notable for a series of extraordinary events. It begins with a bang, usually with an amazing occurrence, and the end of the year often brings a repeat of the astonishing event that started it. This year is favorable to any who would take a calculated risk. It is favorable to those who think big and are prepared to work toward their goals. It must be remembered that the dragon does not favor the idle or those who avoid their responsibilities. Many people will feel that fate has taken a hand in their lives in the dragon year.

It is said that in the year of the earth dragon, nature itself will become turbulent, so earthquakes and cataclysms are to be expected. Fortunately, we don't have to worry about that until 2048.

The Fortunes of the Dragon Year by Year

The Dragon in the Rat Year: The rat loves the dragon, so the dragon can expect happiness and appreciation this year. The dragon's love life will bring joy and security while the domestic situation will be comfortable and contented. The dragon will be flattered and fêeted, amused and adored. In fact, the only concern this year is a tendency to be an outrageous spendthrift.

The Dragon in the Ox Year: The traditionalist ox is no friend to the innovative dragon, so this could be a fairly dismal year. The usual dragon sparkle is muted, and a headlong reliance on luck is not advised. The dragon must think before acting because fortune does not favor the bold. In the ox year, the dragon must grudgingly bide his or her time.

The Dragon in the Tiger Year: The tiger is the dragon's friend, so this is beneficial to financial fortunes and there is a taste for adventure in this year. The dragon is likely to achieve great things and may also be rewarded for a courageous act. However, dragons must guard against arrogance or being too ready to bask in the limelight, or they'll have cause to regret their boastfulness.

The Dragon in the Hare Year: The dragon is incompatible with the hare, so this is likely to be a boring and difficult year. The dragon's exuberance and enthusiasm will be unappreciated, and that is a hard thing for the proud dragon to bear. So dragons must be prepared to step back, watch their manners, and quietly make steady, unassuming progress.

The Dragon in the Dragon Year: This is a make-or-break year that will herald a series of challenges for dragons. While it is true that there are plenty of opportunities for the dragon to excel, there are likely to be a lot of hurdles to get over as well. Fortunately, the dragon will be particularly charismatic at this time and finances should be on the increase too. Dragons in the dragon year must show the world what they're made of and prove that their grandiose ideas are worthwhile.

The Dragon in the Snake Year: The snake is compatible with the dragon, so this year should be fortunate. However, the snake favors those who are subtle, so it will be a wise dragon who knows when to keep his or her opinions close to the vest. The dragon is likely to benefit from other people's mistakes and may develop a deeper understanding of human foibles and frailties. He or she should not to be distracted by petty politics and power plays.

The Dragon in the Horse Year: Fate takes a hand in the dragon's affairs this year, and abundant good fortune ensures that this is going to be a fast and furious, exciting ride. This is a year for adventure and for dragons to enrich their life experience. Dragons shouldn't allow their good fortune to go to their heads and should curb any tendency to act in a superior manner to those less fortunate than themselves.

The Dragon in the Sheep Year: The inspiring sheep urges the dragon to express his or her boundless creativity. Dragons who work in the media, the theater, or the arts will do very well, but even those who have more conventional careers will find new talents. Negative influences will leave the dragon's life, and new companions who appreciate the dragon's gifts will be welcomed.

The Dragon in the Monkey Year: The unpredictable monkey year could make the dragon feel insecure. This might be a good thing, though, as it will prevent the dragon from charging blindly ahead into disaster. Dragons shouldn't be too proud to admit to a mistake or change a course of action that they know instinctively to be wrong. On a more positive note, the monkey adds excitement and variety to the dragon's love life.

The Dragon in the Rooster Year: The rooster is a friend to the dragon, but he demands total candor, especially in relationships. This could be bad news for the dragon's love life and could make the dragon question his or her emotional commitments. On the other hand, the dragon's career and finances will do well, ensuring personal security long after this year has ended.

The Dragon in the Dog Year: The dog demands total fidelity, and the flighty dragon will find that this is a difficult time in his or her love life. The truth is that the dragon will find it impossible to be selfish and will learn grudgingly to put the interests of others first. He or she may well benefit in the long run from this selflessness, but it will still create unease in the dragon's character.

The Dragon in the Pig Year: The pig admires the dragon, so this is a very lucky year with astonishing successes in every sphere of the dragon's life. Now the dragon will find the appreciation, not to say adulation, that he or she has sought! However, it would be wise to keep that arrogance in check or the dragon could squander all the goodwill that has been built. A little modesty while the dragon is at the pinnacle of success will gain a lot of respect.

9

THE SNAKE

THE SNAKE

1941, 1953, 1965, 1977, 1989, 2001, 2013

The Symbolism of the Snake

The snake is considered to be the sign of wisdom. The snake is wise, glamorous and cunning, beautiful and elegant. It is important to remember that when dealing with a snake there is always an underlying hint of a threat.

The Virtues of the Snake: Amiable, honorable, fun-loving, sympathetic, philosophical, fashionable, charitable, intuitive, diplomatic, sexy

The Vices of the Snake: Arrogant, conniving, clinging, pessimistic, ostentatious, a very sore loser

The Snake Personality

Those born in the year of the subtle snake are usually intelligent, decisive, stylish, and eloquent. Easily bored by repetitive activities, snake personalities love variety in everything that they do. A lover of stimulating debate, a snake person will not tolerate idle chatter for long before moving on to something infinitely more interesting. The snake is a quick and accurate judge of situations and people. Snakes usually look beneath the surface and soon have a very good idea of what is going on in the most complex issue and indeed the most complex person. The snake person will make a good friend but an unforgiving enemy.

The Snake in Love

The snake personality is an independent one. Snakes rarely feel the need for other people's approval and regard it as beneath them to take other people's views into consideration.

A snake's greatest dread is to become totally dependent on someone else. Secondary to that, to appear foolish or weak would be almost as shameful. So it can be seen that the snake personality requires a very forgiving partner, one who will appreciate the foibles of an essentially eccentric character. However, the snake is sexy and sensual, and these traits will prove an attractive lure to a prospective mate.

The snake personality is very seductive and very attractive. Snakes are most suited to the candid rooster, whose insistence on telling the truth will captivate this serpent. Perhaps the snake doesn't find it necessary to pretend to the rooster. The diligent ox is also considered a most compatible lover. The snake finds the ox's strength very attractive.

Snakes will make friends with those of their own sign as well as winning the appreciation of rats, hares, dragons, sheep, and dogs.

The overly sentimental pig will irritate the snake, who will open his jaws wide to devour the poor creature. The tiger is odious to the snake. According to traditional Chinese belief, "Should the snake catch sight of the tiger, it is as if he were wounded with a knife."

The Snake Career

Snakes are logical and organized workers who possess the patience that is required to acquire many skills. The snake is capable of swiftly understanding and then competently handling the most complex situations. The snake will go about his or her duties in a quiet, controlled manner—preferably operating alone, with little outside interference. In financial terms, snake people are often very lucky, sometimes coming into money through inheritance, divorce settlements, winnings, or unexpected strokes of luck.

Professions that would suit the snake's character best include politics, public relations, psychologist, entrepreneur, philosopher, archaeologist, and astrologer. However, any career that involves traveling and a varied range of new activities would suit the snake well.

THE SNAKE AND THE FIVE ELEMENTS

The five traditional Chinese elements also have an influence on those born under the sign of the snake.

The Wood Snake (1965)

The wood-snake person often has a difficult start in life. He or she may suffer early ill health or experience poverty and is therefore cautious and conscious of personal security throughout life. The wood snake has a subtle mind and is fascinated by intrigue and the dark byways of history. This is a very witty snake, who hates crowds and messiness. The wood snake is vain, especially about his or her hair. In affairs of the heart, the wood snake is attractive, seductive, and very fickle.

The Fire Snake (1977)

The fire snake has a huge personality that is impossible to ignore. A dominant force, the fire snake is self-possessed, arrogant, and opinionated. Usually found in the company of influential people, this is an extremely ambitious snake who may yet regret the choices made and the price paid to fulfill his or her desires. In love, the fire snake is a little too self-centered for comfort.

The Earth Snake (1989)

The earth snake is extremely determined and never loses sight of his or her long-term goals. A hard worker, the earth snake is considered fortunate. He or she is likely to have conservative opinions and regard order and precision as the supreme virtues. Canny and lucky in business matters and property dealings, the earth snake is likely to become wealthy. In love, the earth-snake person may appear callous, yet this type needs a loving and understanding companion.

The Metal Snake (1941, 2001)

A metal-snake person is extremely talented and has unique gifts, yet eccentricities, lack of firm direction, pride, and capacity for deception can lead to unpopularity. It is too easy for a metal-snake character to alienate potential allies. If one can get past the formidable defenses, metal snakes will become good and loyal friends, though they are equally likely to become unforgiving and underhanded enemies. Male metal snakes are usually attracted to younger women, while the females of this sign are drawn to influential older men.

The Water Snake (1953, 2013)

The water-snake personality is fastidious, astute, intelligent, and pragmatic. It could be said that water snakes have a lateral view of life and a sly, wry sense of humor. Happiest when slithering through the corridors of power, water snakes are ambitious, charming, and lucky. Not noted for emotional declarations or outbursts, this snake is an intellectual and prefers the company of those who are also mentally alert.

THE YEAR OF THE SNAKE

The snake lives in hollows and under stones, so in its own year it's no surprise that some of these stones will be over-turned. This year casts an eye on many questions and mysteries that haven't seen the light in a very long time. Politicians and national governments will feel the full glare of the serpent's merciless gaze, and we can be sure that the cunning serpent will not rest until every scandal is rooted out and all mysteries revealed.

More generally, the snake favors those who are patient and subtle; however, people who are rash and impetuous will have cause to regret their thoughtless haste.

The snake is an inventive sign, so this will be a year for innovations. Remarkable scientific breakthroughs and astonishing discoveries are due at this time. At the same time, the stylish elegance of the snake will find a reflection in the arts and the world of fashion. New trends in fashion, music, film, theater, and TV are very likely.

The Fortunes of the Snake Year by Year

The Snake in the Rat Year: This will be a trying year for snakes. Sudden changes are likely to play havoc with the snake's emotions, and even though the financial outlook is quite good, the snake could well be left wondering why he or she bothers while struggling to find enough money to go around! All in all, this is one year when snakes will feel generally harassed.

The Snake in the Ox Year: The ox is a fortunate sign for the snake, but even so, the slow, plodding pace will be a little wearing. Money worries are likely to occupy the snake's attention at the Chinese New Year, and snakes will wonder when their financial troubles will ease. They can take comfort, because the ox, though slow, is steady and sure, and as the year progresses the snake will see gradual improvements. It's just a matter of staying cool and keeping one's head.

The Snake in the Tiger Year: Life will again pick up speed for snakes during this year. The naturally slow, steady serpent will struggle with this, especially during the early months, as foolish accidents cause a loss of face. The snake should just try to go with the flow, because life will move more smoothly the less the snake struggles!

The Snake in the Hare Year: The year of the stylish hare will prove a relief to the fraught snake. The refined pace of life will suit the snake much better, and frustrations will soon ease. At last, snake personalities will feel more confident and will soon find both the time and the money to enjoy life's pleasures. It's a great time to get out more, to see a little more of the world, and to do it in style!

The Snake in the Dragon Year: Although this will be a year full of bluster and dramas, the snake will be thankful that these dramas will tend to affect other people. This is an ideal time for snakes to slither off into a hole and avoid these problems. Remember that no matter how well intentioned snakes are, they can't take care of everything and they have to get their priorities right. In the dragon year, self-interest and self-preservation are not bad things.

The Snake in the Snake Year: Opportunities will come knocking for snakes during their own year. Fortunately they will be more than ready to make use of them; whatever has been dreamed of in the past will now be made possible if snakes can find the determination to make it all happen. This is also a good time to pour oil on troubled waters, as old arguments will now be forgotten and life will become more peaceful!

The Snake in the Horse Year: Snakes will find the year of the horse a rather difficult one to cope with. The usual subtle tactics won't work, and it would be best for snakes to avoid far-reaching legal transactions or business dealings because very little will go according to plan. The snake must try to be honest and open in his or her dealings because it will be all too easy to have one's motives misunderstood or misrepresented.

The Snake in the Sheep Year: If the snake's motivations were called into question in the horse year, then the opposite applies in the year of the sheep. Untrustworthy and unscrupulous people might try to worm their way into the snake's life by playing on his or her emotions. A wise snake will be extremely cautious and take extra care. After all, more than money may be lost, and the snake's ability to trust might be a casualty of this emotionally difficult time.

The Snake in the Monkey Year: Although snakes enjoy a little intrigue, the chaos of the monkey year could cause more confusion than is comfortable. Snakes are likely to spend an enormous amount of time struggling to figure out what's really going on. They must make an earnest attempt to not get involved in anything that doesn't affect them directly, even if this means lowering their standards to stay out of trouble!

The Snake in the Rooster Year: The rooster is a friend of the snake, and although there might still be a few problems to iron out, this will be a much better year for snake people. Plans will move a step closer to becoming reality as new friends and allies will offer practical help. With a bit of luck the snake might even find new love! All in all, the rooster year should provide a boost to the snake's income and ego.

The Snake in the Dog Year: Snakes tend to fare well in the year of the faithful dog. The financial and practical side of snakes' lives will see improvement, and it is likely that snakes will find themselves in an exciting new job or running a new and profitable business. A word of caution: snakes must remember that life is about more than hard work and worldly success. Snakes should also find some time to enjoy them-selves, to combat mounting stress levels.

The Snake in the Pig Year: Some species of snake, such as the python, are capable of swallowing a pig whole, so it's not surprising that snake personalities will want immedi-ately to consume all the opportunities this year brings. Snakes will feel more in control this year; some might move house or give their old one a makeover. Although the picture looks rosy, the snake should try not to be too greedy or too impulsive. The only real thing to beware of is the danger of being led astray by a close friend or lover.

10

THE HORSE

THE HORSE

1930, 1942, 1954, 1966, 1978, 1990, 2002, 2014

The Symbolism of the Horse

The horse is considered the sign of ardor because passions play a big part in this impetuous steed's life. Subsidiary interpretations of the horse's character include a strong possibility of the establishment of a distinguished career. In Chinese tradition, the horse represents nobility.

The Virtues of the Horse: Productive, warmhearted, enthusiastic, amusing, industrious, agreeable, sociable, logical, strong-minded

The Vices of the Horse: Defiant, unscrupulous, opportunistic, moody, self-serving, unwilling to listen to reason

The Horse Character

Horse personalities are cheerful, independent minded, outgoing, and often outspoken, and they are usually very popular on account of their immense charm. Easily affected by the moods of others, horses thrive in the company of lively, cheerful people. They usually rise to the occasion, amusing their audience and inspiring passions with their eloquent words. On the other hand, if the horse does not receive the appreciation he desires from those around him, then he is likely to become moody, impatient, and sarcastic.

The genuine enthusiasm of the horse's personality will easily win friends who will want to confide their deepest secrets to this noble equine. It is here that the basic fault of the horse character becomes evident. It is a sad truth that the horse finds it almost impossible to keep tight-lipped, especially if the secret is particularly juicy. A horse person born in the winter months is said to be luckier than one born in summer.

The Horse in Love

Horse personalities love to be in love. Often caught up with the thrill of romance, the impulsive horse is exhilarated by new relationships, sometimes to the point of forgetting existing responsibilities as he or she happily races into forging new, tempestuous emotional links. Of course, in youth this trait does lead to some scrapes, so horses have generally been around the track a few times before they settle down. However, the horse can be tamed by soothing words, genuine affection, and a demonstration of tenderness.

Those best suited to a long-term relationship with a spirited horse are the ever-faithful dog, the refined and talented sheep, and the courageous tiger. The horse enjoys lively company, so the friendships of dragons, snakes, monkeys, roosters, and pigs are most agreeable.

The horse won't be so comfortable in the company of the opportunistic and devious rat or the snobbish hare. The ox may be too slow and precise for the exuberance of the horse, and according to Chinese tradition, "The white horse cannot share a stall with the black ox." This means that a horse person who happens to be born in a year governed by the metal element should never marry a water ox.

The Horse Career

Most horse personalities possess a strong sense of responsibility and will work very hard on behalf of their families and dependents. Horses are noted for astonishing stamina. Horses can work, party, or athletically push their physical boundaries until everyone else has collapsed with exhaustion. Horse people are also clever with their hands. Being so active, it is no surprise that the horse personality is a restless one, and many born under this sign are great travelers. The careers best suited to the horse personality include the construction worker, sportsperson, explorer, geographer, actor, artist, dress designer, engineer, sales-person, and advertising executive.

THE HORSE AND THE FIVE ELEMENTS

The five traditional Chinese elements also have their part to play, adding to the characteristics of the horse.

The Wood Horse (1954, 2014)

The element wood adds an affinity for the natural world to the spirited horse personality. The wood-horse type usually prefers country life to the urban sprawl. He or she is friendly, sociable, and cooperative. The wood horse's mind is filled with ideas about how to improve things, and this type may have little time for traditional values and practices. The wood-horse person is intelligent and freedom loving and has the capacity to recover from adversities.

The Fire Horse (1966)

The fire horse is wild, and traditional Chinese thought regards this type with dread, because this personality is often a little too hot to handle. That said, this type is flamboyant, charismatic, ingenious, and clever. However, the fire horse is rebellious, with moods that are likely to be extremely volatile causing this personality to suffer difficulties in trying to establish a stable relationship. The fire horse loves travel and can be a thrill seeker.

The Earth Horse (1978)

The earth horse is very logical, possibly too much so, because the tendency to weigh everything for a considerable length of time makes this type indecisive. Even after thinking things through, the earth horse is often left in a morass of confusion and in need of the guidance of others. This innate insecurity may be concealed by a tendency to act in a bossy manner. The families of earth-horse people aren't very helpful, so friends frequently take the place of relatives. When youthful, this is a wild horse, but this type tends to mature well.

The Metal Horse (1930, 1990)

The metal horse is a stubborn, self-centered horse who is noted for his restlessness, love of variety, and thrill-seeking nature. Never boring (and indeed fearing boredom), this type rarely settles down long enough to establish stable relationships. This horse is nevertheless exciting company. It is fortunate that the metal-horse character can usually afford to live the good life. Not afraid of controversy or arguments, this horse loves to show off and actually enjoys shocking others.

The Water Horse (1942, 2002)

Early life for the water horse is likely to have been difficult. This type is emotionally very vulnerable and hates noisy arguments or being surrounded by chaotic lifestyles. It is this trait that will enable this personality to become very successful. The water horse is very competitive, often a traveler, and physically strong and adventurous. A water horse is a great listener and an eloquent, persuasive communicator. This type's close relationships may cause problems because he or she finds it easy to make promises but far more difficult to fulfill them.

THE YEAR OF THE HORSE

The year of the horse is one in which those who are enterprising and prepared to work hard toward their goals will do very well. Think of the horse year as a bucking bronco who will kick and jump, dart from side to side, and generally try to throw its rider. All the rider has to do is hang on. Those who can be flexible and take advantage of every opportunity will prosper, while those who give up at the first buck will gain nothing except a few bruises. Plans that have been made in previous years will now come to fruition; however, schemes that are off-the-cuff or not well thought out will toss you from the saddle with no warning.

The horse year favors those of honest, independent attitudes with a sense of flair. The sense of integrity becomes more important because secrets come out in the horse year and revelations are all too common, so scandalous celebrities and dubious politicians had better beware.

The Fortunes of the Horse Year by Year

The Horse in the Rat Year: The year of the cunning rat is likely to be a trying time for honest and straightforward horse personalities. All that scheming and deceit is distressing, and it could lead to feelings of insecurity and worry. Caution should be a wise horse's watchword, because it would be too easy to be befuddled by fast talkers. A horse should put his or her own plans on hold; otherwise, he or she will end up fighting battles on all fronts!

The Horse in the Ox Year: The year of the placid ox should be a far more comfortable one for horses. Being in the company of another grazing animal will tend to make this a better year all around. Although this year will bring a lot of hard work, at least horses will feel like they are getting somewhere and that their efforts will eventually be rewarded. On the other hand, the horse's love life this year may be quite turbulent.

The Horse in the Tiger Year: The prospects for a horse's finances will definitely improve during the year of the daring tiger. However, it is this very urge to be adventurous that could prove to be the horse's undoing. Although many opportunities will present themselves, the horse must take care not to be overconfident or to leap into a situation before all the ramifications are fully understood. The same message applies to prospective relationships.

The Horse in the Hare Year: An excellent year is forecast for horses, as they feel the need to widen horizons and make their mark on the world. Some horse personalities might take this literally and embark on a career that puts them in the public eye. Even if horses do encounter a few green-eyed enemies, they shouldn't worry, because they won't be able to take a wrong step!

The Horse in the Dragon Year: The positive influences of the zodiac continue for fortunate horse personalities in the year

fsimply chinese astrology

of the exuberant dragon. Horses will be productive, capable, efficient, and successful. The horse's social life will also prosper, and a renewed sense of fun and adventure will add to the excitement. The only downside is that the horse's notorious tactlessness might come to the fore, so if he or she can manage not to offend too many people along the way, it will be a great year!

The Horse in the Snake Year: The levelheadedness of the horse personality seems to take a vacation in the year of the sensuous snake. The practicalities of life will tend to be ignored as temptation rears its attractive head again and again. Most horse personalities will find that resistance is futile—not that they will try very hard. However, it would be wise to at least try to stay on the straight and narrow, because fantasy is likely to overcome realism this year.

The Horse in the Horse Year: Oddly, horse personalities do not often enjoy the experience of the horse year. It's a case of coming back to reality with a bump, and many will find the going quite tough at times. However, even though things will be a struggle, horse personalities will learn valuable lessons along the way. There are indications of a new life path opening, but not quite yet! The horse should hold back on making any life-changing decisions until things settle down a little.

The Horse in the Sheep Year: After the struggles of the previous year, the year of the sheep will seem much easier. Life will enter a period of relative calm, and horse personalities will notice gradual improvements in both the career area and love life. Many horse people will consider this to be the perfect time to abandon a nomadic lifestyle and settle down!

The Horse in the Monkey Year: As might be expected, the year of the fickle monkey is one of novelty and fun for horse people. There are plenty of opportunities around if horses are quick off the starting line and if they can keep up the hectic pace. If the horse is feeling particularly adventurous, then he or she may opt for a gamble or two. That's not to say that all of them will pay off, but the horse will add to his or her store of experience and will probably have a lot of fun along the way.

The Horse in the Rooster Year: The judgmental rooster demands a little more responsibility from the horse personality. Sensible decisions are favored, while fickleness and a wayward spirit are not. With this in mind, the rooster year is particularly favorable for the formation of a committed partnership. It is equally good for large investments such as the purchase of a new home. Horses must be prudent now and plan carefully for the future.

The Horse in the Dog Year: This year, the horse will not be in the character of a racer, but in a more humble aspect as the hardworking plough horse. The faithful nature of the dog demands that the horse put loyalty to others first, so it would be an unwise horse who acts in a selfish manner. On the other hand, the dog is favorable to relationships, and many horse personalities will now be content to share their feelings.

The Horse in the Pig Year: The equine love of taking risks is severely restricted in the year of the timid little pig. This is not the time to give in to sudden impulses or take silly chances. There will be far too many complications and variables to take a chance, so a wise horse will be extra cautious, even if prospects seem to be good. The horse must plan each step and pay more attention to personal security this year.

11

THE SHEEP

THE SHEEP

1931, 1943, 1955, 1967, 1979, 1991, 2003, 2015

The Symbolism of the Sheep

As well as being another animal symbolic of agriculture and fertility, the sheep is also considered to be the sign of art. In its youthful form as a lamb, this sign is also an emblem of filial piety. In ancient China, the sheep was a common sacrificial animal; it has therefore come to represent an uncomplaining acceptance of fate.

The Virtues of the Sheep: Compassionate, easygoing, gentle, sweet-natured, creative, artistic, affectionate, fashionable, disliking strict discipline

The Vices of the Sheep: Overly emotional, pessimistic, insecure, indecisive, overly dependent, troubled in love life, with erratic mood swings

The Sheep Personality

The personality of someone born in the year of the sheep is likely to be thoughtful and studious but often reserved or even shy. Sheep people are kindly, good-natured, patient, and reliable. This is a dutiful, hardworking type of person, capable of taking on an enormous workload. However, this trait could be the sheep's downfall, because although the sheep can cope with the pressure for a while, he or she must be careful that overworking doesn't result in sickness from stress-related complaints. Naturally creative, sheep people have artistic, somewhat dreamy minds and deeply sensitive souls. This sensitivity is so delicate that sheep personalities will evolve a sort of psychological armor by putting on a display of apparent indifference. This is an effective disguise, but don't be taken in, because no one is softer or more caring than the sheep. Bearing this in mind, it is easy to see that sheep characters loathe confrontations and are easily embarrassed by anything vulgar or brash.

The Sheep in Love

Sheep are attractive people even when their natural insecurity causes them to doubt this fact. They have a superb sense of style, a natural grace, and an appealing, yet unassuming, personality. The best side of the sheep character is found in their caring, loving attitude. Their values are based on a spiritual rather than a material plane, and they are totally lacking in envy or malice. With these characteristics, it is easy to see why the sheep is likely to be in demand and considered to be a worthy mate by so many people.

The talented sheep is particularly drawn to those of a similar creative or original nature. It is easy to see that happiness is likely to be found with the horse, the refined hare, and the sympathetic pig.

The sheep's unassuming nature will enhance his or her popularity, especially with those born under the signs of the tiger, dragon, snake, monkey, or rooster, and with other sheep.

Pessimism is a sheep's enemy, and many internal battles will be fought to maintain a positive frame of mind, so it is not surprising that other signs who are also prone to negative thinking will not do the sensitive sheep any favors. The ox will be left far behind by the sparkling imagination of the sheep. The sheep will be plunged into a pit of gloom by the dog and made to feel totally inadequate by the go-getting rat.

The Sheep Career

The sheep is considered to be a fortunate sign, and people born under this artistic and original sign have the ability to turn a bleak, unpromising situation into a glittering success. Rigid schedules and tiresome routines are to be avoided, because the sheep has an easygoing nature and needs variety in his or her working life. This is not a particularly ambitious sign (sheep people hate the anxiety of competition, so early success is unlikely) but once that perfect niche has been found, the sheep will find professional happiness.

Sheep personalities often work in the arts, the media, as writers, or in professions involving health care. Chinese tradition says that sheep were the treasurers of the ancient courts, and it is true that these people have a deft touch with accounting and the complexities of taxes and bureaucracy.

THE SHEEP AND THE FIVE ELEMENTS

The five traditional Chinese elements give extra variations to the sheep's character.

The Wood Sheep (1955, 2015)

Fair play and honorable conduct are the hallmarks of the wood sheep. This is a deeply thoughtful person who tends to be nostalgic, sentimental, and good-humored. However, this type may be too trusting and thus can be taken advantage of by less scrupulous people. There will always be someone around to help the wood sheep out when in need. Whatever sex the sheep is, he or she will tend to "mother" loved ones.

The Fire Sheep (1967)

The fire sheep is not so much a sheep as a ram! The fire sheep is courageous, ready to take the initiative and defend his or her territory. The artistic side of this sheep will express itself as a love of drama. However, this type will not be so fortunate with money and is in danger of mismanaging his or her affairs. This is probably because the fire sheep is something of a wishful thinker and daydreamer.

The Earth Sheep (1979)

Even though the hardworking earth sheep could be described as neurotic, defensive, and literal, this type has many positive traits. He or she is straightforward, trustworthy, and stable, with a streak of sensitivity. This is a sheep who will gain prosperity through his or her own efforts. The earth sheep is extremely creative and happiest when he or she can share tastes with like-minded people. The earth sheep loathes deceit and so may be too honest for comfort, especially within a relationship.

The Metal Sheep (1931, 1991)

A sheep person born under the influence of the metal element has more confidence than most other sheep in the flock and has a highly refined artistic sensibility and an honorable nature. Even so, the ego is still vulnerable and this type can be easily hurt. The metal sheep is also moody and can be prone to becoming so possessive as to fall prey to jealousy. This type is clannish and very family oriented and may avoid social situations among strangers.

The Water Sheep (1943, 2003)

A sheep influenced by the water element is desperate for love and approval and will do anything to get it! The water sheep is very sensitive, hates to upset anyone, and will usually be content to meekly follow the flock. This is a most unassuming, humble sheep, who prefers not to attract too much notice. As this type ages, his or her shyness fades and the water sheep blooms. Then he or she will become an excellent communicator, easily loved and admired but still much too modest.

THE YEAR OF THE SHEEP

The year of the sheep is a good one for world peace. The sheep loathes confrontations, so international difficulties are likely to be resolved or to at least come to a truce in this period. It is equally likely that philanthropic, humane people will rise to positions of power at this time and that they will reform corrupt institutions. Traditionally, the year of the sheep favors anything that will benefit humanity, so social and medical advances are likely.

The artistic side of the sheep is likely to find expression in radical new fashion trends and mass movements, especially those that promote peace. The year of the sheep is a good one in which to marry or to breathe new life into a flagging relationship. If a parting of the ways is contemplated, the outlook is not so good, simply because the family-oriented sheep disapproves of immorality and divorce.

The Fortunes of the Sheep Year by Year

The Sheep in the Rat Year: Money can't fail to be a top priority in the rat year, with the sheep's anxiety reaching a fever pitch. The important thing is not to take any risks with cash. If a sheep is in doubt as to whether he or she can afford something, the answer is, probably not! There's too much temptation to be resisted, but a wise sheep will hold back because the day of reckoning will surely come.

The Sheep in the Ox Year: If a sheep has built up debts in the previous year, then this demanding time will see him or her working hard to pay them off. Those sheep people who resisted temptation can now put their efforts into more productive areas and set some firm foundations for their future. The ox is not exactly a friend to the poor sheep, so fun is thin on the ground, but at least the sheep will learn some valuable lessons.

The Sheep in the Tiger Year: The year of the demanding, arrogant, and adventurous tiger could be a difficult one for the sheep's anxiety levels. This is a complex time, and the sheep will need to keep his or her wits. There will be too many ups and downs for comfort. It will be very difficult to feel secure. This is a time when a wise sheep will be more unassuming than usual, staying in the background and avoiding fuss.

The Sheep in the Hare Year: The refined hare is compatible with the sheep, so there is an injection of fun and laughter this year. The sheep's social graces will be enhanced, and taste and artistry will be appreciated. All of this adds up to a time when the sheep will be the person to know. The sheep will make new and influential friends. In financial terms, this year is mediocre, but that is more than made up for by the boost to the sheep's ego and popularity.

The Sheep in the Dragon Year: The beginning of this year will be excellent for the sheep. The sheep loves flair and style, and the dragon has an extraordinary amount of it. The imagination will be stimulated, and sheep people will be happier and more carefree. The last quarter of the dragon year might present some minor financial worries, so a wise sheep will have put something away for a rainy day.

The Sheep in the Snake Year: Anything requiring talent and flair is favored in the snake year, so the creative sheep should be happy at this time. Sheep will be appreciated for their qualities and talents, so feelings of insecurity or inadequacy will be banished. The sheep will also be very persuasive and will be able to talk his or her way to an advantage. Romantically speaking, this is one of the sheep's best years.

The Sheep in the Horse Year: A sense of safety is welcome to the sheep as the horse year brings some material security. The sheep's knack for creative thinking will make life easier. Originality will be appreciated, and the sheep will gain a great deal of respect for the inventive solutions that he or she comes up with. Travel is well starred in this year.

The Sheep in the Sheep Year: All the sheep's efforts over the past twelve years will be rewarded when they enter their own time period. The sheep can be himself, free from the complaints, demands, and criticisms of others. The more usual anxieties and insecurities will be muted if not forgotten now, and this alone will add to the sheep's personal charisma. In this year the sheep will gain the confidence to make far-reaching, life-changing decisions.

The Sheep in the Monkey Year: It is impossible to be bored in the year of the monkey, and for the sheep, that's likely to be the best thing one could say about it! There is an old Chinese curse that states, "May you live in interesting times," and these times will be too interesting for comfort for a sensitive sheep. It would be foolish in the extreme for the sheep to take risks or to be too trusting in the unpredictable, ever-changing scenarios that this year will bring.

The Sheep in the Rooster Year: The sheep's overdeveloped sensitivity could be quite battered by the outspoken candor of the rooster. The sheep's delicate ego will be devastated if he or she doesn't keep a low profile this year. It is too easy to be discouraged and to believe that everything is just too difficult and beyond the sheep's capabilities. This is not so, because while this will be a challenging time, a persistent sheep will get through this and come out a stronger person.

The Sheep in the Dog Year: This is likely to be a year that is notable for self-denial and austerity. It's unlikely that any sheep will enjoy that experience. The sheep's need for reassurance may be ignored now simply because other people are too busy with their own concerns to be overly sympathetic to the sheep's sensitivities. A wise sheep will forget his or own needs for a while and find a new purpose in helping others in a charitable venture of some kind.

The Sheep in the Pig Year: The friendly and sensitive pig signals a time conducive to the sheep's creative nature. It is also good news because the sheep will be able to indulge his or her taste for luxury. Others will appreciate the talented and imaginative sheep this year. This is a time when good fortune will find the sheep, but even so it is important that the sheep recognize his or her limits. As long as the sheep don't push their luck, and moderate their demands, they will do very well.

12

THE MONKEY

THE MONKEY

1932, 1944, 1956, 1968, 1980, 1992, 2004, 2016

The Symbolism of the Monkey

The monkey is traditionally called the sign of fantasy. To the Chinese, this mischievous, resourceful, and intelligent simian is thought of as the likable trickster, Sun Wu-Kong, the monkey king in the epic tale "Journey to the West." The familiar imagery of the "three wise monkeys," namely, "hear no evil, see no evil, speak no evil," is of Japanese origin.

The Virtues of the Monkey: Lively, complex, humorous, agile, diplomatic, charming, flexible, excellent memory, resistant to insults, competitive

The Vices of the Monkey: Dishonest, sarcastic, lacking respect, jealous, prone to temptation, restless

The Monkey Personality

Fast thinking, witty, and exciting, monkeys yearn for a life of constant variety that is filled with new and stimulating people. The monkey's ever-active mind means that he or she is quickly bored, and the monkey loathes the company of boring people. Monkey types are rarely guilty of being boring themselves. They are often very intuitive and quick to catch onto a new idea. Their highly developed intuition skills allow their unconscious minds to operate independently of their conscious thoughts. They can therefore answer any question swiftly and think about several things simultaneously. It is this trait that has led them to be accused of being tricky customers. Monkeys also possess a quick and ready wit. This can express itself as withering sarcasm, which is one of the monkey's less appealing features.

The Monkey in Love

Monkeys are attracted to the excitement of being in love. This does not mean that they are in love with any one person but that they like the idea of being in an ardent romance. It is very likely that those born under this sign experience a lively love life with any number of partners. Potential mates are drawn to the monkey character by its charm, good humor, openness, and endless curiosity about the world. Once in a relationship, the monkey personality can occasionally be unpredictable or even childish, but it just adds to the excitement and variety. Needless to say, the person who embarks on a long-term relationship with a monkey must be openminded and very tolerant. Once trust is gained, the monkey will prove to be a supportive, if unconventional, partner. Even when a relationship ends, monkeys are very good at retaining the friendship and affection of former lovers.

The monkey character is very compatible with those born under the signs of the audacious rat and the glamorous dragon.

The monkey will dazzle and make friends easily with those born under the influence of the dog, the sheep, and the hare.

The monkey's sense of humor does not impress the snake, the pig, or the tiger.

The Monkey Career

The versatility and quick-wittedness of the monkey make this type suitable for a wide variety of jobs. Those with the character of nimble simians can resent those in positions of authority, and they lack the kind of deference that employers tend to expect. Monkey personalities do not naturally gravitate to work in large organizations. By nature, monkeys are highly self-reliant and self-motivated. Monkeys are capable of hard work as long as they can set their own goals, which they will achieve at their own swift pace. The monkey is unconventional and creative, and so tends to be drawn to a career in the media, public relations, design, and the arts. Some monkeys take to supervisory roles or become skilled manual workers, craftspeople, surveyors, and planners.

THE MONKEY AND THE FIVE ELEMENTS

Each of the five traditional Chinese elements has an influence on the complex monkey character and adds significance to the interpretation of the sign.

The Wood Monkey (1944, 2004)

The element of wood enables the monkey to achieve stability and success, but only after the restlessness and desire for an exciting and unsettled life are shaken out of his or her system. The wood-monkey personality eventually develops into a streetwise, canny, and shrewd individual who is rarely afraid of anything. Wood monkeys need firm guidance from a partner. Conscious of this, the wood monkey will spend a lot of time looking, and a lot of time being disappointed. It is logical, therefore, that a later marriage will be more successful than the earlier, more ardent and impulsive partnerships.

The Fire Monkey (1956, 2016)

The fiery type of monkey personality is extremely imaginative, active, and energetic. This type can usually be detected by a habit of constantly gesticulating. This bold monkey is naturally bossy. To be fair, the fire monkey is a natural leader who can motivate all those in the vicinity. However, this type can be prone to rashness and will have cause to regret any impulsive actions. The fire monkey is stubborn and opinionated, constantly right (in his or her own opinion), very competitive, and prone to unfounded suspicions.

The Earth Monkey (1968)

The earth monkey is the most calm and quiet personality of all those born under this sign. Generous and protective to loved ones, this type is totally unfeeling and cold to the needs of people who are at a distance. In common with other monkey types, the earth monkey is mentally agile and knowledgeable—and quietly but insistently demands that all who live and work nearby appreciate the fact. This type can, like other monkeys, be roguish and charming, imaginative and clever. If the fire monkey applies his or her talents to one endeavor at a time without being distracted, then this type will enjoy great success.

The Metal Monkey (1980)

Although the metal element often gives an outwardly cool, sophisticated, and independent image, the reality is that this monkey is a passionate, possessive, ambitious, creative, and hardworking personality. The metal monkey will do things his or her own way and hates to be advised or directed (tending to interpret this as nagging). This type is creative and intelligent but too conscious of his or her own image and too superior for his or her own good. The metal monkey has a strong belief system and is a profound thinker.

The Water Monkey (1932, 1992)

The watery nature of this chattering monkey ensures that he or she is a charming diplomat and superb negotiator. It is not surprising, therefore, that this monkey is often found in the role of go-between, as an agent or business representative. This is a shrewd, self-willed, capable, and attractive character, bold, eloquent, and stylish. Extremely curious by nature, this type will travel extensively and make influential friends on every continent. Water monkeys usually tend to marry into money and position; not only that, but they also develop a good relationship with in-laws. On the other hand, water monkeys are easily offended, and they mask their insecurities by a barrage of charming words.

THE YEAR OF THE MONKEY

In the year of the monkey the world is ready for everything that is novel, unusual, and downright eccentric. Ideas that would not have been given the time of day in previous years will now be joyfully considered. The monkey year is not the best one in which to make long-term plans. The very nature of the monkey is unpredictable, so the best-laid plans will go awry—often before they've even started. Adaptability is the key to success this year, because the wheel of fortune is spinning wildly. Quick profits can be made but also lost in swift succession. Nervous types would be well advised to keep their heads down and not take chances, while the rasher and more enterprising types take all the risks. Romantic inclinations fare better—but even this area will be subject to erratic variations. Those who are flirtatious will have a marvelous time, but for those who prefer a more settled relationship, the outlook is more anxious.

The Fortunes of the Monkey Year by Year

The Monkey in the Rat Year: The rat and the monkey are compatible signs, so this should be a fortunate year for all monkey personalities. If monkeys have felt that they were missing out on the big breaks in previous years, the time of the rat will be very welcome and will provide opportunities very swiftly. Finances are favored, as is a monkey's love life. All in all, this is a positive and progressive year.

The Monkey in the Ox Year: The ox approves of hard work and diligent effort. Although the monkey is capable of sustained effort, the need to stick to the rules may sometimes be a little hard to bear. Even though the opportunities will come a monkey's way, this type is unlikely to feel too enthusiastic about them. Most monkeys will find the ox year somewhat dull. However, it does provide the chance to learn a few new skills that will be useful in the upcoming tiger year.

The Monkey in the Tiger Year: Even though in personal terms the monkey and the tiger don't get along, this year should provide some unexpected strokes of luck. The only real danger is that a monkey might take his or her luck for granted and become complacent and lazy. The clever monkey will be much in demand as an adviser at this time.

The Monkey in the Hare Year: Happiness is likely to be found in the compatible year of the hare. There is a chance to relax and allow all tensions to fade away, and the monkey will feel more at ease. This is also a chance to reassess, consolidate, and realize that the monkey has reached a reasonably good position. Romance should flourish and the monkey's influence should grow. This is a very good time to ask for favors.

The Monkey in the Dragon Year: As long as the ever-curious monkey is prepared to put effort into improving his or her education, the year of the dragon should be a good one. This is a time to express ambition and to extend one's experience. Travel to distant lands in order to broaden knowledge is worth doing. However, this is also likely to be an expensive year, so monkeys should be cautious in the use of their resources.

The Monkey in the Snake Year: A monkey had better be nimble in the year of the snake to avoid being caught in its treacherous coils. There are many dangers in this year, and a wise monkey should curb the chattering to avoid making enemies or talking him- or herself into trouble. The monkey's love life especially is prone to serious complications if he or she is not very careful.

The Monkey in the Horse Year: The horse year is another in which caution should be the monkey's watchword. Individualism is not encouraged at this time, and the monkey may feel constricted by rules, regulations, and respectability. The financial situation is not at all promising, so the monkey must take extra care in dealing with assets and debts.

The Monkey in the Sheep Year: The sheep year arrives with a sigh of relief because it give monkeys a chance to sort out their lives and put the difficulties of the past behind them. A creative approach is finally appreciated, and monkeys will feel more content as they swiftly solve their problems one by one. If the monkey is mindful of past errors, then he or she is assured of prosperity. By the end of the year, the monkey should be fairly well off but should not flaunt his or her good fortune.

The Monkey in the Monkey Year: In the monkey's own year this type reveals his or her true nature. The monkey has boundless curiosity, chatters constantly, and possesses a staggering capacity to handle the most complex issues. Thoughts of duty and responsibility are cast aside as monkeys set out with one aim in mind: to enjoy themselves. Even though it's probably the last thing on a monkey's mind, any enterprise started this year is likely to be a roaring success.

The Monkey in the Rooster Year: As long as a monkey does not believe everthing he or she hears in this year, all will be well. It's a good idea to develop a slight sense of suspicion, to question assumptions, and to be a little wary. This is also a time when a monkey should weigh the relative importance of friends and associates and treat them accordingly. It would also be a good idea to pay a little more attention to family matters.

The Monkey in the Dog Year: The year of the dog is likely to be a dismal one for monkey personalities. The fun seems to have been drained from life as responsibilities and financial anxieties occupy more and more of the monkey's time. Relationships bring problems because everybody seems worn down by worry and is too preoccupied to pay much attention to the monkey's concerns. The best traits a monkey possesses are resilience and the determination to get through this trying year.

The Monkey in the Pig Year: The green-eyed monster of envy could become an unattractive addition to the monkey's personality this year, as everyone else seems to be doing well while the monkey is left behind. This is not true, but it will be easy for the monkey to feel that way. The fortunate year of the rat will come in after this dull year, so monkeys will work and plan for a time when luck will smile on them again.

13

THE ROOSTER

THE ROOSTER

1933, 1945, 1957, 1969, 1981, 1993, 2005, 2017

The Symbolism of the Rooster

The rooster is considered to be the sign of candor, and the rooster symbol is regarded as a potent charm to ward off evil: "The cock frightens demons, who flee at the sight of his red comb." Chinese tradition holds that the rooster is endowed with five "virtues": an intelligent mind that is shown by his crown, a martial spirit that is revealed by his spurs, courage that never backs down from a fight, benevolence because he cares for the hens, and finally, reliability because he always crows at sunrise.

The Virtues of the Rooster: Intelligent, perceptive, honest, excellent memory, alert, organized, generous, attractive, a confident performer

The Vices of the Rooster: Boastful, show-off, opinionated, critical

The Rooster Personality

Those born under the sign of the rooster have an exhibitionist streak. In Chinese tradition, roosters were thought to be military types, probably because they like impressive dress uniforms, medals, and banners. Today there are a disproportionate number of roosters in the media, where they can show off and get paid for it! Even if a rooster is not in the public eye, he or she likes to be in the spotlight. Impeccable grooming and individualistic dress sense often characterize the rooster. Many will criticize the rooster for flamboyance and a carefree manner, but these traits may mask a well-concealed shyness. Rooster personalities are independent, surprisingly sensitive, wise, compassionate, and brave. They never shirk duty, they are confident in their own judgments, and they can be straightforward to the point of being insulting, even though that is the last thing they intend.

The Rooster in Love

The rooster is a charmer, although many will consider this type's manner brash and forward. There are bound to be many romantic opportunities in this type's life, and it will be a rare rooster who does not have a harem of "hens" in the background. Boredom is the rooster's great enemy, so this type is likely to move on to more congenial company if a partner becomes too predictable. The rooster's essential independence keeps this personality on the move, at least in early adult life, but this rule of freedom is not applied to others. In fact, roosters have a jealous streak, which they try to keep well hidden. The female born under the sign of the rooster is usually far more practical than the male, and she is far more impressed by old-fashioned responsibility.

Though this may make the rooster sound fickle, it is not the case. Indeed, while the rooster may go to great lengths to give that impression, he (or she) is actually capable of deep commitment to an interesting and responsible partner. The necessary stability in close relationships is likely to be found with those born under the signs of the snake, the ox, and the dragon.

The rooster's sense of style wins appreciation from tigers, horses, sheep, monkeys, and pigs. The truthful and straightforward rooster hates the hare's snobbery and the rat's opportunism. Tradition holds that two roosters cannot share a house in harmony and that "the cock sheds tears at the sight of the dog."

The Rooster Career

Roosters are logical thinkers, but they hate to be pressured or forced to make instant decisions. Their independent streak leads them to prefer working alone at their own pace. This will lead to great productivity, and they can find creative, workable solutions to problems. Needless to say, many roosters are suited to self-employment. If a rooster is micromanaged by others, he or she will feel trapped and become overcritical of his or her own efforts. This scenario can lead to depression.

The rooster is capable of great, if individualistic, success and can make a lot of money. However, the rooster is liable to spend it as quickly as he accumulates it. Roosters are particularly suited to the media, public relations, commercial sales, and politics. Many become authors, entertainers, and beauticians. Others follow Chinese tradition and become career soldiers.

THE ROOSTER AND THE FIVE ELEMENTS

The five traditional Chinese elements also have a bearing on the rooster personality.

The Wood Rooster (1945, 2005)

Wood roosters are optimists even when their chances seem slim, and this most often pays off. The wood rooster is very demanding but fair, decent, and honest. The wood element makes the rooster very passionate, not just in an amorous sense (although he or she will be very ardent) but also in terms of pet subjects. This rooster is so communicative that he or she could talk his way to a gold medal in an Olympic event.

The Fire Rooster (1957, 2017)

The intense, talented, persevering, excitable, and self-motivated fire rooster is destined for the top! This independent-minded rooster, a natural leader who will easily attract followers whether he intends to or not, is going to be noticed. This type's charm ensures that he or she will make many friends from different walks of life. This rooster's financial fortunes will increase with the years.

The Earth Rooster (1969)

The earth rooster is quick on the uptake, with a thought process that is systematic and analytical. An excellent organizer, this type is better than most roosters when it comes to controlling money. The earth rooster, however, can be prone to mood swings and be very opinionated. The earth rooster desperately needs emotional security and may marry young to find it in order to escape the pressures of his early family life.

The Metal Rooster (1981)

The addition of metal will tend to make this rooster more abrasive than other types. Metal roosters are very idealistic, hardworking, and determined. However, they have notoriously sharp tongues and are considered difficult and moody. If ever a spokesperson were needed, the metal rooster is the perfect candidate. This type is capable of tying the opposition in knots by skilled and eloquent arguments spiced with some devastating observations. Also, there is no chance of the metal rooster's giving up until victory is ensured.

The Water Rooster
(1933, 1993)

The water rooster is undoubtedly the great communicator. This type simply loves to talk, gossip, and share any piece of information that comes within earshot. Indiscretion is this rooster's middle name. The water rooster is at home with any form of communication—writing, computing, and, of course, verbal dexterity! This type is a superb organizer and persuader. The water rooster has refined taste and loves art and music.

THE YEAR OF THE ROOSTER

The confidence of the rooster should be infectious this year. This is a time when it is right to accept challenges and push the boundaries a little. Like this personality's friend the monkey, the rooster is fond of innovation, so this year provides another chance to air ideas that are unusual, unorthodox, and even outrageous. There will be a new interest apparent in these strange ideas, even if they have been previously rejected.

The year of the rooster is good news for anyone who wishes to advance at work, achieve a higher status in society, or achieve prominence in any creative field. The rooster brings a sense of order and organization, so where there was chaos, a new era of order will be established. This will be a new set of workable rules, but in affairs of the heart, some partnerships will be put under strain. This is probably because one partner starts to assert a more independent attitude and the terms of the relationship suddenly change.

The Fortunes of the Rooster Year by Year

The Rooster in the Rat Year: This is not the best year for roosters, and they should restrain any impulse to take risks even if the chances seem on the surface to be very good. Even if roosters make profits, it is doubtful that they will be able to keep them for long. The only way that roosters will prosper this year is if they are sensible, plan their moves carefully, make sensible decisions, and err on the side of caution.

The Rooster in the Ox Year: The ox is a compatible sign, so the rooster will be happier this year. Although the ox period calls for hard work, and favors must be earned this year, the rooster's plans will not be obstructed—in fact, many opportunities are bound to come the rooster's way. Common sense is in fashion this year, so as long as the rooster does not allow the heart to rule the head, all will be well.

The Rooster in the Tiger Year: This will be an exhausting year. Even though roosters like action, the hectic pace and revolutionary fervor that is in the air will be enough to wear out even the most energetic fowl. Many roosters will soon have enough of the party and wish to retire in seclusion, but their pride won't allow that, so it's a matter of soldiering on until the end is achieved.

The Rooster in the Hare Year: Even though the rooster and the hare don't really get along, the calmer atmosphere of the year of the hare should soothe the rooster's nerves. This is not a year for roosters to puff up their feathers. They should stick to whatever is familiar and be happy with small successes. Practical matters will go well, even if unspectacularly. Romantic inclinations are likely to be unsatisfying.

The Rooster in the Dragon Year: This is a chance for the rooster to show off in the year of the flamboyant dragon. The rooster should make quite an impression and receive a lot of approval. This is a good time to begin anything new. It is an excellent year for establishing a lasting relationship, marrying, or opening a business.

The Rooster in the Snake Year: Good fortune continues into the year of the snake. The rooster and snake are compatible, so romance is well starred. The confidence of the rooster personality will win favor, and it will be permissible for roosters to be self-assertive and to draw attention to their accomplishments. This is bound to create some envy, but roosters will be so happy that they simply won't care.

The Rooster in the Horse Year: Roosters have a right to feel optimistic in the horse year, even if there are a few financial hurdles in the path. Hard work is required to solve the problem, so it's a good thing that roosters are not idle. Wise roosters will look after their health now, ditch some bad habits, eat sensibly, and exercise more.

The Rooster in the Sheep Year: There are far too many mysteries for the rooster to sleep soundly in the confusing year of the sheep. Small matters seem to expand into problems of staggering size, and too much energy will be expended on trifling details. Roosters should try to control their anxiety levels and not be too self-critical. After all, little is asked of roosters this year, so they should at least try to relax a little.

The Rooster in the Monkey Year: This is a chaotic year, so the rooster's instinctive desire for order is bound to be offended. It should dawn on the most obsessive of roosters that no amount of careful planning is going to make the slightest difference, because this is a time when fortunes can change in an instant. As long as a rooster is adaptable, then all will be well. Just go with the flow and don't make a fuss.

The Rooster in the Rooster Year: Roosters can enjoy themselves in their own year. While they are having a good time, they can also plan their next moves and get things started with the confidence that they will ultimately succeed. The roosters' bank accounts may be a little stretched, yet the former's capacity for hard work will ensure that they will soon make up any losses. All the rooster traits will be appreciated now, so roosters should display their feathers and crow.

The Rooster in the Dog Year: In contrast to their own year, roosters are likely to find the year of the dog rather dull. It seems that the entire period consists of unrelenting effort with very little reward. Roosters will also be in demand by everyone, sometimes for weird reasons and usually at the most inconvenient moments.

The Rooster in the Pig Year: The rooster will find his or her tolerance tested time and again in the pig year. The rooster knows instinctively that effort is required to gain anything worthwhile, so when things come along too quickly and easily, an element of skepticism and distrust gnaws at the edges of the rooster's mind. It may be that he or she is being too suspicious, but it is hard for the rooster to know exactly what is going on. The rooster will have to wait to find out whether the promise of the pig year will be fulfilled.

THE DOG

THE DOG

1934, 1946, 1958, 1970, 1982, 1994, 2006, 2018

The Symbolism of the Dog

The dog is valued for its fidelity and is considered to be the sign of wisdom and loyalty. Pekingese dogs were held in such high regard that their breeding was strictly regulated by the imperial household. The so-called Buddhist lion is actually a palace dog. Statues of these watchful beasts were set up at temple entrances as symbolic protectors.

The Virtues of the Dog: Moral, with high standards of behavior, warm natured, respected, possessed of a strong sense of justice, a good listener, a faithful friend, able to spot hidden dangers

The Vices of the Dog: Anxious, pessimistic, often hot-headed, too critical of love partners

The Dog Personality

Those born under the sign of the dog have an honest and courageous nature. These are natural crusaders, ready to fight for a worthy cause and to defend their friends and family to the last breath. It is easy for a dog personality to empathize with the feelings of others and to identify with other people's causes and ideals. There is a strong sense of justice here, and a dog person will quickly become offended if he or she feels that someone else is being taken advantage of or beaten down. This trait is very evident to other people, and they will repay the dog's loyalty with respect and trust. It is a very rare dog who will break a promise or betray a confidence.

It is probably because dog personalities have such a high sense of moral values that they can become hypercritical of both their own behavior and that of others. The strong sense of duty also obliges them to point out others' weaknesses and failings with alarming regularity.

The Dog in Love

Although the dog is not the most glamorous sign in the Chinese zodiac, people born under the influence of this faithful animal will be very attractive, not least because they are good listeners and are extremely loyal. However, it will take a lot of coaxing to persuade these canines to reveal their inner feelings, because they are wary of burdening others with their anxieties. Dog people need a lot of encouragement and reassurance, so they enjoy the company of a more confident and adventurous partner. A person with a turbulent spirit would be hateful to the dog, who prefers a more reliable and less emotionally intense mate. In romance, the dog prefers to start with a friendship and allow it to grow, because he or she hates to be rushed into anything. When a relationship has been established, a dog must try to control negative thoughts and not be oversensitive to a partner's incidental remarks.

The faithful dog will be happy with the adventurous spirits of the tiger and horse as well as with the refinement of the hare. The dog's innate kindness and fidelity will be appreciated by the rat, snake, monkey, pig, and, of course, other dogs.

The ox will add to the dog's neurosis and plunge the canine into a pit of gloom. The sheep has a knack of making the dog feel inferior, while the rooster will get on the dog's nerves. Worst of all, the dragon's excessive enthusiasms will worry the dog.

The Dog Career

This is, above all, a responsible and trustworthy sign, so dogs will often be found in positions of authority and in possession of sensitive information, which they divulge to no one. Dogs are happiest when their roles are clearly defined and their responsibilities clearly understood by everyone. Dog personalities tend to avoid competitive, aggressive professions and prefer to work as part of a team in a steady, controlled, and productive manner. Once a dog has made a commitment to a project, a course of action, or a career path, he or she will follow it with conscientious attention to detail and determination in order to make it as much of a success as possible.

Dog personalities are particularly suited to a career as teacher, lawyer, social worker, doctor, nurse, counselor, campaigner, or member of the clergy.

THE DOG AND THE FIVE ELEMENTS

The five traditional Chinese elements add another set of interpretations to the trustworthy dog personality.

The Wood Dog (1934, 1994)

The genuinely popular, generous, and amiable wood dogs are certainly house-trained. Very domestic and family oriented, they are often experts at do-it-yourself projects, decorating, and gardening. They derive spiritual strength from their families. They tend to be honest, considerate, and cooperative. According to Chinese tradition, wood dogs must be on guard against strangers and take precautions against theft.

The Fire Dog (1946, 2006)

The addition of the fire element ensures that this dog possesses a flair for the dramatic. The fire dog tends to be lucky and possessed of the ability to make a mark in the world. This type is charming, more adventurous than most other dog types, and scrupulously honest. This dog will have a good reputation and will be protective of his or her family. More independent than other canines and occasionally rebellious, the fire dog enjoys travel and novelty.

The Earth Dog (1958, 2018)

The earth dog is an idealist. Efficient in everything and respected for wise and impartial advice, this dog is methodical and an excellent organizer of his or her own affairs and the activities of others. The earth dog may be quite secretive and is a persistent worker, often wearing him- or herself out because he or she never seems to feel the need to take a rest. Periodic financial problems are a recurring feature in the life of the earth dog because, despite this type's natural caution, there is a spendthrift tendency.

The Metal Dog (1970)

The idealistic dog nature reaches an extreme when combined with the metal element. The metal dog has a dominant personality and is most often found in a position of prominence and authority. Some metal dogs are quite tyrannical and very touchy, constantly on the lookout for people or things to be offended by. As usual, this dog is devoted to family and can be a faithful friend. A metal-dog person is at his or her best when crusading for a worthwhile cause.

The Water Dog (1982)

The water-dog personality will make friends easily because he or she is very attractive, amusing, charming, and sympathetic. This type is a very good listener, and an intuitive understanding of human nature will help the water dog to empathize with others. The water dog loves travel, meeting new people, and doing fascinating things. Too restless to settle down in early life, later the water dog will adore his or her family. Water dogs easily make influential friends.

THE YEAR OF THE DOG

The ever-vigilant dog sounds a warning of danger in this year. It is a timely reminder that one should ensure the security of one's home and possessions. This note of caution will apply to taking gambles too. The sign of the dog is cautious by nature and warns against taking too much on faith or going too far out on a limb. The time of brash self-confidence has gone, so this is a time to be extremely sensible. Finances should be invested in something reliable, solid, and—let's face it—boring! No resources should be risked on vague promises or apparently spectacular schemes—they are literally too good to be true. The dog year is good news for relationships, and a marriage in this year will ensure a lifetime's devotion and fidelity.

The Fortunes of the Dog Year by Year

The Dog in the Rat Year: The year of the rat is one of overt materialism, and this may offend the dog's finer feelings. Even though dogs will observe a lot of injustice in this period, it will be difficult to do anything about it, so wise canines will bide their time. Dogs aren't too happy in the rat race and will be more content if they can get as far from it as possible.

The Dog in the Ox Year: The all-embracing concentration of practicality that an ox year demands has little attraction for the idealistic dog. Any crusading zeal or revolutionary fervor will be out of fashion for a while, so it would be best for the dog to toe the line, fit in as much as possible, and not be too disruptive.

The Dog in the Tiger Year: This should be a more comfortable period for the dog, because the tiger will welcome the dog's revolutionary zeal. The dog and the tiger often think alike, and the dog will be happy, bounding away and enjoying the fast and furious pace of events. The dog's self-esteem will grow, and victory is assured in any conflict. However, dogs will be more gullible than usual so they should be careful whom they believe and not allow themselves to be led astray by wishful thinking.

The Dog in the Hare Year: The hare flees from the dog, and it is usual for the beginning of the hare year to be a complete waste of time. There's far too much running around and pursuing something that is impossible to catch. Wise dogs will tell themselves not to be so excitable and will endeavor to develop a calmer, more philosophical attitude. The dog's advice will be much in demand, and as the hare year progresses, romance is favored.

The Dog in the Dragon Year: The dog had better be prepared to take second place in the year of the dragon. It's a time of reassessment and learning, and it would be a good idea for the dog to accept good advice. Every experience in the dragon year will add to the dog's knowledge, and he or she will get a chance to apply this new wisdom in the future.

The Dog in the Snake Year: The sly snake is a disturbing influence to the loyal dog. There are too many upheavals for comfort, and the number of intrigues and deceptions will add to the dog's anxieties. To achieve anything worthwhile this year, the dog must apply lessons learned and be more assertive. However, it is important that the dog maintain his or her integrity and refuse to be drawn into any shady dealings.

The Dog in the Horse Year: The year of the horse is likely to be filled with minor problems, and this fact alone will keep dogs on their toes. As long as a dog personality can maintain self-confidence and keep to the planned course, then all will be well. However, if the dog allows doubts to become overwhelming, success will not be achieved. Even though this is likely to be an anxious time, the dog's material fortunes should slowly improve.

The Dog in the Sheep Year: The year of the sheep is good news for the dog's amorous prospects and it is also favorable for any artistic and creative interests. That's the good news! However, dogs will still be prone to anxieties, especially concerning money. It is certain that the dog will achieve considerable triumphs this year, but even victories will cause more worry. Let's face it: dogs are worriers!

The Dog in the Monkey Year: Fortune favors the brave in the monkey year, and those dogs who can overcome their

146

innate caution and take a small gamble will prosper. It's a good year for travel, expanding personal horizons, and romance. Any sector of a dog's life that has been unsatisfactory will be boosted by an unexpected stroke of luck.

The Dog in the Rooster Year: This year is likely to represent a lesson in reality. The dog's lofty idealism must take second place when harsh practicalities need to be addressed. This is not to say that basic values will be lost, but rather that the canine will have to bow to the prevailing necessities and get down to the nitty-gritty.

The Dog in the Dog Year: In his own year the dog will be gratified that many of his or her ideals will be appreciated and put into practice. Dogs will meet with good fortune and others will appreciate their finer qualities. At last, the world will be ready to hear the dog's views and to act on them. Dog personalities will be praised, and although it is not in the nature of dogs to believe flattery, they can at least allow themselves a few moments of self-congratulation.

The Dog in the Pig Year: The pressure eases in the year of the pig, and although canines don't usually allow themselves any downtime, the happy-go-lucky pig year might force them to do just that. This period provides an antidote to stress, and even dogs will have to admit that they could do with a little bit more fun. This is a great opportunity to enhance the more cultural, poetic side of the dog's personality.

15

THE PIG

THE PIG

1935, 1947, 1959, 1971, 1983, 1995, 2007, 2019

The Symbolism of the Pig

The pig is considered to be the sign of honesty. It represents wealth, family fortune, and abundant possessions. The domestic pig is therefore considered to be a good omen in China, especially when it is covered in mud. If a traveler should spot a pig on his or her left-hand side, it is said to be a sure indication that the traveler's objective will be attained soon. If the animal is on the traveler's right, then there is still a long way to go.

The Virtues of the Pig: Honest, making a virtue of simplicity, straightforward, pure spirited, diligent, calm, understanding, gallant

The Vices of the Pig: Gullible, easily swindled, willful, obstinate, can be lustful and depraved

The Pig Personality

The happy-go-lucky pig will attract popularity by his or her open attitude and affectionate nature. The pig is also sought after because when anyone is in need, it is invariably a person born under the sign of the kindly pig who will offer assistance and emotional support. Pig personalities are often thought to be reserved when they are first encountered, and this is because they are emotionally vulnerable and they need time to gain confidence with strangers. However, as time progresses, a warm and cheerful character emerges. Pigs have few close friends with whom they shares their thoughts, even though their circle of acquaintances will be wide.

There is an innocence and naivety in the pig personality, which, though attractive, can also put this personality in danger of being conned, swindled, and otherwise deceived. This trait, combined with eagerness for novelty, makes pig personalities yearn for new experiences and encourages them to travel widely.

It is this eagerness that can make pigs tactless or encourage them to behave in an inappropriate manner. Even so, it is easy to forgive pigs simply because they have no malice.

The Pig in Love

It is in the area of romance that pig personalities are at their most vulnerable. It is necessary for them to experiment, to be outgoing and meet potential mates, but there is the ever-present danger that these people are unsuitable and self-seeking, or willing to take advantage of the pig's good nature. It is a good thing that pigs are quick learners and rarely make the same mistake twice. At least when a suitable partner is found, the pig will be absolutely sure that this is indeed the right one!

Pig personalities are very tolerant and will be quietly amused by the personal foibles of their partners, but never make the mistake of thinking that pigs have not noticed what is going on. They may seem to be dreaming their lives away, but they are actually very observant. The pig needs someone who will share a sense of fun, as well as recognizing this type's more serious and sensitive side.

The pig is likely to find love with the refined hare and the artistically gifted sheep. The pig's natural charm will win approval from most signs, particularly the rat, ox, tiger, dragon, horse, rooster, and dog.

It is not considered wise for pigs to consort with other pigs because a sense of paranoia will emerge. The snake will take advantage of the pig's good nature, while the monkey and pig have very little in common at all.

The Pig Career

Pigs are not traditionally thought to be very ambitious and they are happiest when they have established a good equilibrium between home and work. Of course, pigs are capable of competent work, but they prefer to find a comfortable rut and stay in it, rather than scaling the stressful ladder of success. A pig finds it preferable to work in cooperation with others as part of an efficient team. Pigs are methodical and like to know exactly where they are. Risks make pigs extremely nervous, so there is a tendency to err on the side of caution.

Pigs are suited to a career in medicine, teaching, or the caregiving professions. The law or music may appeal to some, while others will prefer a more scientific role. Pigs find satisfaction as writers, landscape gardeners, artists, librarians, computer programmers, or researchers.

THE PIG AND THE FIVE ELEMENTS

The five ancient traditional Chinese elements impart an extra dimension to the tolerant pig character.

The Wood Pig (1935, 1995)

The wood-pig personality is a conventional one. The usual pig characteristics of tolerance, intelligence, and modesty are in evidence. This is a compassionate pig who is always ready to help others who are less fortunate. This may be accomplished by cleverly manipulating people around to the pig's way of thinking. However, the pig's tendency to be gullible is also present. Wood pigs often excel at athletics or writing.

The Fire Pig (1947, 2007)

The fire-pig personality can be described as possessing an artistic temperament. This person tends to be highly strung, a little eccentric, intensely emotional, and possessed of strong intuition; the fire pig can sometimes be quite psychic. The caring or medical professions attract fire pigs, but some are more drawn to alternative therapies. This type of pig is very popular, cheerful, fun-loving, and devoted to family. Fire pigs tend to worry about relationships and finances. Under stress, the fire pig can be obstinate, willful, and something of a bully.

The Earth Pig (1959, 2019)

Earth pigs are sensible pigs who pride themselves on their sound common sense and steady, productive habits. The earth-pig type is not usually very ambitious and may rely on a tougher and more pragmatic partner. The earth pig wants to lead a quiet, ordinary, uncomplicated life. This pig is devoted to family and indeed to family values. This type is careful with money, but that does not stop the earth pig from being extremely fond of food and drink.

The Metal Pig (1971)

The metal pig is the most ambitious individual born under this sign. Indeed, this type can be forceful, domineering, and determined to get his or her own way. The metal-pig personality is more extroverted than the usual pig and can be extremely sociable, but always keeps something back from acquaintances. This type can be moody and certainly needs periods of solitude. Emotionally, this pig is possessive and very protective of friends and family.

The Water Pig (1983)

The water pig possesses a dreamy nature and is creative and artistic. Watery types of pigs don't mind some financial insecurity as long as they can express their creativity and be allowed the peace to dream. As might be imagined, this type is very sensitive, romantic, and caring, and so emotional as to be easily upset. Water pigs love travel and can regale an audience with tall tales of their adventures. This pig is not ambitious, but is very sensuous and prone to overindulge.

THE YEAR OF THE PIG

This is the last of the animal signs, so it can be taken as a celestial message to tie up loose ends, come to terms with all that has happened in the previous twelve years, and prepare for a new beginning. It may be a period marked by nostalgia and a few regrets. That said, it is important that positive influences and events be paramount. In other words, the pig year is one in which every one of us can assess how far we've come, count our blessings, and consider our next moves. Of course, those who have squandered their opportunities throughout the animal-sign cycle may think very differently now.

In essence, there is a feeling of celebration, and in common with the symbolism of the fun-loving pig, this could be a time for self-indulgence and enjoyment of the finer things of life. The kindly pig also looks with favor on romance, so amorous adventures will be fortunate. Family affairs and domestic issues will prove to be favorable.

Even though anything as strenuous as political upheaval is unlikely, there may still be a revolution in ideas and concepts in the pig year. However, this change is most likely to occur in leisure activities and may bring a change in the way that vast numbers of people spend their recreation time.

The Fortunes of the Pig Year by Year

The Pig in the Rat Year: There should be optimism in the air while the pig takes a successful path in the year of the friendly rat. However, it is important for the pig to resist complacency, because the rat favors the enterprising and the bold. The pig should pick a goal and slowly aim at it Results may not be immediate, but the eventual rewards will be very great indeed.

The Pig in the Ox Year: The year of the ox calls for hard work, and fortunately the pig is up to the task. Even though there will be some hardship along the way, the outlook is still good. As long as the pleasure-loving side of the pig's personality doesn't gain dominance, there is a lot to be gained this year. So all a wise pig has to watch out for is a tendency to alienate colleagues by overindulging.

The Pig in the Tiger Year: The turbulent year of the tiger is not a comfortable one for the often-timid pig. All the revolutionary

changes are very unsettling even when the pig actually sympa-
thizes with the aims. To avoid anxiety, the pig should stand
back, follow his or her own concerns, and try to let the world's
events pass by. This attitude will ensure popularity, for the pig
will be much sought after, and the pig's laid-back personality
will provide respite for others in this fraught time.

The Pig in the Hare Year: The outlook for the pig's cash
reserves looks pretty good in the year of the hare. Of course,
with all this extra affluence, the self-indulgent pig can afford a
more opulent lifestyle, and he or she will be determined to get
one! The pig must take care not to be overgenerous, though.
The pig's personality gains some strength this year, so this
type will be able to stand up for him- or herself and cut a more
forceful figure during this twelve-month period.

The Pig in the Dragon Year: Financial good fortune continues in the ostentatious dragon year. However, the pig
may feel ill at ease and even a little guilty that everything
seems to be going his or her way while other people suffer.
Many pigs have a suspicion that something underhanded
and sneaky is going on, and even worse, that they are an
unwitting part of it. Pigs will also feel that times are about
to change and that there may be some payback up ahead.

The Pig in the Snake Year: Caution is the watchword in the
year of the pig's enemy, the snake. Nothing is straightforward
or as it seems to be. No business deal will be aboveboard and
no relationship will be emotionally sound. It is going to be an
anxious time for the pig.

The Pig in the Horse Year: The pig's fraught nerves can relax
in the year of the horse. The pig can use this time to recu-
perate. During this period, there will be a lot of analysis and

self-doubt, but the pig's fortunes are rising. Pigs thwarted in love find that situation changing rapidly for the better.

The Pig in the Sheep Year: The pressure seems to be off when the year of the sheep comes around. This is not the most exciting of years, but then again, that's exactly the way the pig likes it. Finances will be steady, and heady romance will give way to simple contentment.

The Pig in the Monkey Year: The monkey and the pig are incompatible signs, so this is not going to be one of the better years. There are intrigues going on, and the pig will be hard-pressed to keep up with all their twists and turns. This time may also be too risky for comfort, so a wise pig will take care, make preparations, and hold fast to his decisions and principles.

The Pig in the Rooster Year: The year of the strutting rooster will bring a much needed lesson in economy and financial planning for the pig. It will show that though the best things in life are not necessarily free, they are certainly cheaper. In this period, the pig enters a more controlled phase and develops more cultural, refined tastes.

The Pig in the Dog Year: The year of the idealistic dog may sound promising, but it's too full of well-meaning crusaders to give the pig much peace. Pigs should not be taken in by promises and should demand proof of all claims. The lives of those around the pig will be full of turmoil, so the pig will have to learn to say no and to separate him- or herself from disruptive influences if there is to be any peace at all in the pig's year.

The Pig in the Pig Year: An increase in personal confidence will come as a relief. Fortune smiles on the pig, and plenty of opportunities arise. Many pigs embark on long-term relationships with people who understand this personality and allow their partners breathing space. This emotional link may be a secret affair. Other pigs will move to a new home or start a family. Good fortune decrees financial successes.

INDEX